ASIA BOND MONITOR
MARCH 2021

ASIAN DEVELOPMENT BANK

 Creative Commons Attribution 3.0 IGO license (CC BY 3.0 IGO)

© 2021 Asian Development Bank
6 ADB Avenue, Mandaluyong City, 1550 Metro Manila, Philippines
Tel +63 2 8632 4444; Fax +63 2 8636 2444
www.adb.org

Some rights reserved. Published in 2021.

ISBN 978-92-9262-771-3 (print), 978-92-9262-772-0 (electronic), 978-92-9262-773-7 (ebook)
ISSN 2219-1518 (print), 2219-1526 (electronic)
Publication Stock No. SPR210114-2
DOI: http://dx.doi.org/10.22617/SPR210114-2

The views expressed in this publication are those of the authors and do not necessarily reflect the views and policies of the Asian Development Bank (ADB) or its Board of Governors or the governments they represent.

ADB does not guarantee the accuracy of the data included in this publication and accepts no responsibility for any consequence of their use. The mention of specific companies or products of manufacturers does not imply that they are endorsed or recommended by ADB in preference to others of a similar nature that are not mentioned.

By making any designation of or reference to a particular territory or geographic area, or by using the term "country" in this document, ADB does not intend to make any judgments as to the legal or other status of any territory or area.

This work is available under the Creative Commons Attribution 3.0 IGO license (CC BY 3.0 IGO) https://creativecommons.org/licenses/by/3.0/igo/. By using the content of this publication, you agree to be bound by the terms of this license. For attribution, translations, adaptations, and permissions, please read the provisions and terms of use at https://www.adb.org/terms-use#openaccess.

This CC license does not apply to non-ADB copyright materials in this publication. If the material is attributed to another source, please contact the copyright owner or publisher of that source for permission to reproduce it. ADB cannot be held liable for any claims that arise as a result of your use of the material.

Please contact pubsmarketing@adb.org if you have questions or comments with respect to content, or if you wish to obtain copyright permission for your intended use that does not fall within these terms, or for permission to use the ADB logo.

Corrigenda to ADB publications may be found at http://www.adb.org/publications/corrigenda.

Note:
ADB recognizes "Hong Kong" and "Hongkong" as Hong Kong, China; "China" as the People's Republic of China; "Korea" as the Republic of Korea; "Siam" as Thailand; "Vietnam" as Viet Nam; and "Saigon" as Ho Chi Minh City.

Cover design by Erickson Mercado.

Contents

Emerging East Asian Local Currency Bond Markets: A Regional Update

Highlights	vi
Global and Regional Market Developments	1
Bond Market Developments in the Fourth Quarter of 2020	8
Policy and Regulatory Developments	32
Environmental, Social, and Governance Bonds in ASEAN+3	35
Social Bonds—Recent Developments and Trends	38
AsianBondsOnline 2020 Bond Market Liquidity Survey	44
Market Summaries	
China, People's Republic of	50
Hong Kong, China	52
Indonesia	54
Korea, Republic of	56
Malaysia	58
Philippines	60
Singapore	62
Thailand	64
Viet Nam	66

Emerging East Asian Local Currency Bond Markets: A Regional Update

Highlights

Between 31 December and 15 February, 2-year and 10-year government bond yields in most advanced economies and emerging East Asian markets edged higher on the back of an improved global economic outlook and progress on vaccinations.[1] Optimism over the economic recovery and accommodative monetary stances boosted investment sentiment around the world during the review period.

While most emerging East Asian economies saw their gross domestic product (GDP) contract in 2020, economic performance generally improved in the fourth quarter (Q4) of 2020. Bucking the regional trend, the People's Republic of China (PRC) and Viet Nam posted positive growth in 2020.

Buoyed by the better economic outlook, financial conditions improved. Most regional central banks maintained their accommodative monetary stances to support the fragile recovery. Improved sentiment lifted most equity markets and regional currencies between 31 December and 15 February. Risk premiums were broadly unchanged during the review period. Capital flows into the region's equities and bond markets also recovered in Q4 2020.

Downside risks in 2021 have receded compared to the previous year on the back of the coronavirus disease (COVID-19) vaccine rollouts. However, the uncertain trajectory of the pandemic remains the biggest risk to the global economic recovery. This risk is exacerbated by uneven vaccine rollouts across economies. Another risk is a rise in asset prices due to the increased liquidity generated by central banks in the region. A sudden downturn in equity prices or a reversal in monetary stances by central banks in response to inflationary pressures could destabilize financial markets. One factor in this is the passage of the USD1.9 trillion fiscal stimulus program in the United States, which has raised further concerns of inflation and Federal Reserve tightening. This could cause a pullback of capital from emerging markets.

Emerging East Asia's local currency bond market rose to an aggregate size of USD20.1 trillion at the end of December.

Local currency (LCY) bonds outstanding in emerging East Asia reached USD20.1 trillion at the end of December. Overall growth of the region's bond market slowed to 3.1% quarter-on-quarter (q-o-q) in Q4 2020 from 4.8% q-o-q in the third quarter (Q3) of 2020. On a year-on-year (y-o-y) basis, growth inched up to 18.1% in Q4 2020 from 17.4% in Q3 2020. Emerging East Asia's LCY bond market size expanded to the equivalent of 97.7% of the region's GDP at the end of Q4 2020 from 95.9% in Q3 2020.

Government bonds accounted for 61.8% of the regional LCY bond stock at the end of December. The region's government bond stock reached USD12.4 trillion, posting growth of 3.6% q-o-q and 19.5% y-o-y. Corporate bonds accounted for the remaining 38.2%. The region's corporate bond stock amounted to USD7.7 trillion at the end of December, growing by 2.2% q-o-q and 16.1% y-o-y.

The PRC remained the region's largest bond market, accounting for 77.4% of emerging East Asia's total bond stock at the end of December. This was followed by the Republic of Korea (12.1%) and the aggregate among members of the Association of Southeast Asian Nations (9.0%).[2]

LCY bond issuance in emerging East Asia totaled USD2.0 trillion in Q4 2020. Government bond issuance accounted for 54.8% of the quarterly total and stood at USD1.1 trillion. Government bond issuance declined 23.5% q-o-q but rose 47.3% y-o-y. Issuance of corporate bonds reached USD0.9 trillion, contracting 0.9% q-o-q but expanding 17.3% y-o-y.

The March issue of the *Asia Bond Monitor* includes a box discussing differences between the development of corporate bond markets in East Asia and Latin America,

---

[1] Emerging East Asia comprises the People's Republic of China; Hong Kong, China; Indonesia; the Republic of Korea; Malaysia; the Philippines; Singapore; Thailand; and Viet Nam.
[2] LCY bond statistics for the Association of Southeast Asian Nations include the markets of Indonesia, Malaysia, the Philippines, Singapore, Thailand, and Viet Nam.

and the implications of such differences for financial resilience. This issue also contains three special sections: (i) environmental, social, and governance (ESG) bonds in ASEAN+3; (ii) recent developments in social bonds; and (iii) key findings of *AsianBondsOnline*'s 2020 bond market liquidity survey.[3]

Box: A Comparison of the Expansion of Corporate Bond Markets in East Asia and Latin America

Corporate bond issuance steadily increased in East Asian and Latin American economies between 2010 and 2019. The ratio of corporate debt issuance to GDP rose from 119% to 144% in East Asia and from 34% to 42% in Latin America. In contrast with the common growth trend, bonds were issued largely through domestic markets and in domestic currency in East Asia, while bonds were largely issued in international markets and in foreign currency in Latin America. As a result, Latin America is more vulnerable to changes in global market conditions and currency fluctuations than East Asia.

Special Section: Environmental, Social, and Governance Bonds in ASEAN+3

ESG bonds outstanding in ASEAN+3 markets reached a size of over USD265 billion at the end of December 2020. Green bonds continued to dominate the ESG bond stock, however, their share of the total has declined due to an increase in issuance of social bonds and sustainability bonds. At the end of December, the PRC accounted for the largest share of ESG bonds outstanding in ASEAN+3 markets, followed by Japan and the Republic of Korea.

Special Section: Social Bonds— Recent Developments and Trends

A Primer and Recent Developments in Asia

The ESG bond market has grown significantly over the last few years in response to growing demand. The green bond segment dominates the ESG bond market, with green bond issuance growing to about USD240 billion and social bond issuance reaching around USD150 billion in 2020. Issuance in Asia has been dominated by government-related agency issuers in high-income economies such as Japan and the Republic of Korea. Yet, developing Asia's urgent economic and social development funding needs strengthen the case for a robust social bond market.[4] This section also discusses the impediments to market growth and the regulatory measures needed to further develop the social bond market in the region.

A Nascent Opportunity for ESG Investing

The unprecedented growth of social bonds amid COVID-19 points to the potential of social bonds in financing projects with positive social impacts while also providing new opportunities for institutional investors. Investing in social bonds is beneficial for institutional investors for several reasons. First, the risk–return profile of a social bond is in line with that of a traditional bond from the same issuer. Second, social bonds provide a platform for engagement with corporate issuers. Third, social bonds provide investors with a mechanism to signal their commitment to global social issues and measure the social impact of their investments. Since the market shake-up caused by COVID-19 is expected to persist, investing in social bonds at an early stage will allow institutional investors to support the development of this innovative instrument and reap the benefits of the expected market expansion.

Promoting Social Bonds for Impact Investments in Asia

This section explores how the focus of social bonds has evolved amid the COVID-19 pandemic and contains a detailed discussion on key social areas that could be targeted. A two-pronged approach is proposed to optimize the use of social bonds in financing economic recovery from COVID-19. The approach involves (i) targeting urgent short-term needs such as employment generation, small business support, and healthcare provision; and (ii) funding longer-term programs to reduce poverty and strengthen resilience against future shocks. Lastly, the section touches on the challenges and recent developments in social impact assessment.

---

[3] ASEAN+3 comprises the 10 members of ASEAN plus the PRC, Japan, and the Republic of Korea.
[4] Developing Asia comprises the 46 developing member economies of the Asian Development Bank.

Special Section: *AsianBondsOnline* 2020 Bond Market Liquidity Survey

AsianBondsOnline conducts an annual bond market liquidity survey to review the state of liquidity in the region's LCY bond markets and identify areas of weakness for further development. Overall, liquidity conditions diverged across regional markets in 2020. While most survey participants from the PRC, Indonesia, Malaysia, and Viet Nam noted improved liquidity, those from the Republic of Korea, the Philippines, Singapore, and Thailand observed decreased liquidity. Respondents from Hong Kong, China reported stable liquidity conditions. Survey participants also noted that liquidity was greatly impacted by market sentiment, the global COVID-19 pandemic, and changes in domestic bond yields.

In nearly all markets, government bond turnover ratios declined the most during the second quarter of the year and steadily fell through Q4 2020. On the other hand, movements in corporate bond turnover ratios were mixed in 2020. The survey, which was conducted in Q4 2020, found that bid–ask spreads for government bonds and corporate bonds were largely unchanged from the 2019 survey results.

Survey participants ranked hedging mechanisms for both government bonds and corporate bonds as the most important market development priority, implying a need to expand the availability of hedging instruments. In contrast, settlement and custody scored the highest for both bond segments, reflecting relatively efficient settlement processes across the region's bond markets.

Global and Regional Market Developments

Bond yields rose amid signs of economic recovery and vaccination.

Long-term government bond yields rose in major advanced economies and most emerging East Asian markets from 31 December to 15 February on optimism over the global economic recovery and vaccine rollouts in 2021 (**Table A**).[1] Positive economic sentiment was also reflected in the widening of the spread between 2-year and 10-year government bond yields.

During the review period, 10-year government bond yields among major advanced economies rose, supported by improved economic forecasts. In the United States (US), the 10-year government bond yield gained a significant 30 basis points (bps), while the 2-year yield marginally fell by 1 bp (**Figure A**). In addition to the positive economic outlook, rising yields were supported by expectations of additional fiscal stimulus and ongoing vaccination efforts.

Recent economic data reflect the continued recovery of the US economy. The Federal Reserve noted that gross domestic product (GDP) in the US grew at an annualized rate of 4.1% in the fourth quarter (Q4) of 2020, following a 33.4% gain in the previous quarter. Nonfarm payrolls rebounded in January, with an addition of 166,000 jobs versus a decline of 306,000 in December 2020. In February, nonfarm payrolls further improved, with an additional 379,000 jobs. The unemployment rate fell to 6.2% in February from 6.3% and 6.7% in January and December, respectively. Retail sales also gained 7.6% month-on-month in January after declines of 1.0% and 1.3% in December and November 2020, respectively. The Federal Reserve indicated that investor optimism was high, driven by vaccination efforts and expectations of strong fiscal stimulus.

The Federal Reserve upgraded its GDP forecast in December, raising the forecasts for growth in 2021 and

Table A: Changes in Global Financial Conditions

	2-Year Government Bond (bps)	10-Year Government Bond (bps)	5-Year Credit Default Swap Spread (bps)	Equity Index (%)	FX Rate (%)
Major Advanced Economies					
United States	(1)	30	–	4.8	–
United Kingdom	13	37	(2)	4.6	1.7
Japan	(0.3)	6	(0.03)	8.3	(2.0)
Germany	0.5	19	0.1	2.8	(0.7)
Emerging East Asia					
China, People's Rep. of	10	10	1	5.2	1.1
Hong Kong, China	2	26	–	10.8	0.01
Indonesia	70	36	0.1	4.9	1.0
Korea, Rep. of	(4)	14	0.6	9.5	(1.4)
Malaysia	(0.1)	20	1	(1.2)	(0.3)
Philippines	4	13	2	(2.5)	0.2
Singapore	4	24	–	3.1	(0.1)
Thailand	12	11	2	5.1	0.2
Viet Nam	14	(27)	(1)	1.0	0.4

( ) = negative, – = not available, bps = basis points, FX = foreign exchange.
Notes:
1. Data reflect changes between 31 December 2020 and 15 February 2021.
2. A positive (negative) value for the FX rate indicates the appreciation (depreciation) of the local currency against the United States dollar.
Sources: Bloomberg LP and Institute of International Finance.

---

[1] Emerging East Asia comprises the People's Republic of China; Hong Kong, China; Indonesia; the Republic of Korea; Malaysia; the Philippines; Singapore; Thailand; and Viet Nam.

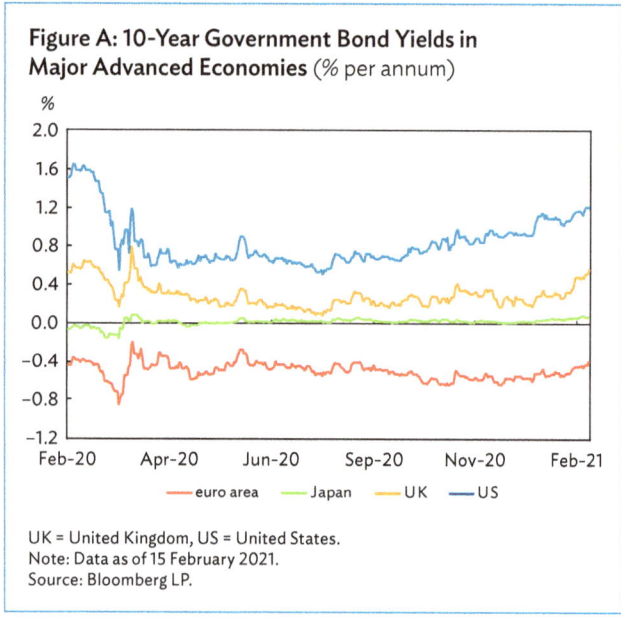

Figure A: 10-Year Government Bond Yields in Major Advanced Economies (% per annum)

UK = United Kingdom, US = United States.
Note: Data as of 15 February 2021.
Source: Bloomberg LP.

2022 to 4.2% and 3.2%, respectively, from 4.0% and 3.0% in September. As widely expected, the Federal Reserve left monetary policy unchanged during its 26–27 January meeting, leaving the federal funds target rate range at 0.0%–0.25%.

The euro area's economy continued to contract in Q4 2020, as GDP declined 4.9% year-on-year (y-o-y) following a decline of 4.2% in the third quarter. Industrial production also declined 0.1% month-on-month in December before rising 0.8% month-on-month in January. Concerns about rising cases of the coronavirus disease (COVID-19) and the emergence of new strains led the European Central Bank (ECB), at its 10 December 2020 meeting, to increase its pandemic emergency monthly purchase program by EUR500 billion to EUR1,850 billion, and to extend the program's end date to March 2022 from June 2021. The ECB subsequently left monetary policy unchanged at its monetary policy meeting on 21 January.

The ECB noted that the pandemic caused a near-term decline in output, while the central bank remained cautiously optimistic over the medium-term amid improving signs for the global economy as well as expanded vaccination programs around the world. In December, the ECB downgraded its 2021 and 2022 GDP forecasts to 3.9% and 4.2%, respectively, from 5.0% and 3.2% in September.

Similar to the US, Japan also posted positive GDP growth in Q4 2020 at 11.7% y-o-y, albeit this was weaker than the 22.8% y-o-y gain in the third quarter. At its 18 December meeting, the Bank of Japan left the monetary policy rate unchanged and extended the duration of its asset purchase program (commercial paper and corporate bonds) by 6 months until the end of September 2021. The Bank of Japan also upgraded its GDP growth forecast for 2021 and 2022 to 3.9% and 1.8%, respectively, from 3.6% and 1.6% in September.

Similar to advanced economies, 2-year and 10-year government bond yields rose in most emerging East Asian markets during the review period. The largest rise in yields came from Indonesia, with its 2-year and 10-year yields rising 70 bps and 36 bps, respectively. Indonesia was one of the earliest regional economies to start a vaccination program. In Q4 2020, Indonesia posted a GDP contraction of 2.2% y-o-y, smaller than the 3.5% y-o-y contraction in the previous quarter. On 18 February, Bank Indonesia lowered its policy rate by 25 bps to support economic growth and downgraded its forecast for 2021 GDP growth to a range of 4.3%–5.3% from 4.8%–5.8%.

Malaysia's 10-year yield gained 20 bps during the review period. At its 20 January monetary policy meeting, Bank Negara Malaysia said that it expected economic growth to recover in the second half of 2021 despite near-term weaknesses. Malaysia's yields were also affected by a ratings downgrade by Fitch to BBB+ from A– on 4 December 2020. Hong Kong, China; Singapore; the Republic of Korea; the Philippines; Thailand; and the People's Republic of China (PRC) all witnessed an increase in their respective 10-year government bond yield. The only exception to the regional trend was Viet Nam, which experienced a 27-bps decline in the 10-year government bond yield that was driven by strong investor demand. However, inflationary concerns are rising due to the unprecedented fiscal stimulus in response to the pandemic, potentially placing further upward pressure on yields. The recent passage of the USD1.9 trillion (8.8% of GDP) fiscal stimulus plan in the US has raised concerns about inflation in the US. Those concerns are evident in rising US bond yields and may prompt the Federal Reserve to tighten policy. Such tightening can potentially trigger capital outflows and financial instability in the region.

In terms of economic performance, all emerging East Asian markets posted contractions in Q4 2020 except the PRC and Viet Nam. The PRC's GDP growth rate rose to 6.5% y-o-y in Q4 2020 from 4.9% y-o-y in Q3 2020, while Viet Nam's GDP growth rose to

Table B: Policy Rate Changes

Economy	Policy Rate 1-Mar-2020 (%)	Mar-2020	Apr-2020	May-2020	Jun-2020	Jul-2020	Aug-2020	Sep-2020	Oct-2020	Nov-2020	Dec-2020	Jan-2021	Feb-2021	Policy Rate 28-Feb-2021 (%)	Change in Policy Rates (basis points)
United States	1.75	↓1.50												0.25	↓150
Euro Area	(0.50)													(0.50)	
Japan	(0.10)													(0.10)	
China, People's Rep. of	3.15		↓0.20											2.95	↓20
Indonesia	4.75	↓0.25			↓0.25	↓0.25				↓0.25		↓0.25		3.50	↓125
Korea, Rep. of	1.25	↓0.50		↓0.25										0.50	↓75
Malaysia	2.75	↓0.25		↓0.50		↓0.25								1.75	↓100
Philippines	3.75	↓0.50	↓0.50		↓0.50					↓0.25				2.00	↓175
Thailand	1.00	↓0.25		↓0.25										0.50	↓50
Viet Nam	6.00	↓1.00		↓0.50				↓0.50						4.00	↓200

( ) = negative.
Notes:
1. Data as of 28 February 2021.
2. For the People's Republic of China, the 1-year medium-term lending facility rate is used. While the 1-year benchmark lending rate is the official policy rate of the People's Bank of China, market players use the 1-year medium-term lending facility rate as a guide for the monetary policy direction of the People's Bank of China.
Sources: Various central bank websites.

4.5% y-o-y in Q4 2020 from 2.6% y-o-y in the previous quarter. To further support economic recovery in 2021, most central banks in the region maintained their accommodative monetary stances, leaving policy rates unchanged during the review period (**Table B**).

However, central banks may begin to tighten monetary policy in response to inflationary pressures. More recently, there are growing concerns about a possible spike in inflation fueled by the massive fiscal stimulus and monetary easing seen in 2020.

Economic Outlook

One big positive shock to the global economy was the advent of safe and effective COVID-19 vaccines in November. The pandemic is far from over, but the good news on vaccine developments and rollouts has lifted business and consumer confidence. Reflecting the positive vaccine developments, the International Monetary Fund (IMF), in its latest *World Economic Outlook Update* released in January 2021, upgraded its global growth forecast for 2021 to 5.5% from an October 2020 forecast of 5.2%. The IMF also estimated that the world economy contracted by 3.5% in 2020. For 2022, the IMF kept its global growth forecast at 4.2%. For advanced economies, the IMF is projecting growth of 4.3% in 2021 and 3.1% in 2022, following an estimated contraction of 4.9% in 2020. The 2021 growth forecast for the US was upgraded sharply in January to 5.1% from 3.1% in October. For emerging markets and developing economies, growth is projected to be 6.3% in 2021 and 5.0% in 2022, following an estimated contraction of 2.4% in 2020.

According to the *Asian Development Outlook Supplement* released in December 2020, developing Asia is projected to grow 6.8% in 2021 after contracting an estimated 0.4% in 2020.[2] The Asian Development Bank's projected 2021 growth figures for the PRC; the Association of Southeast Asian Nations (ASEAN); the Republic of Korea; and Hong Kong, China are 7.7%, 5.2%, 3.3%, and 5.1%, respectively. Relative to the *Asian Development Outlook* released in September 2020, ASEAN's growth forecast was downgraded by 0.3 percentage points from 5.5%, while the other three forecasts remained the same. In 2020, the PRC grew by an estimated 2.1%; ASEAN; the Republic of Korea; and Hong Kong, China contracted by 4.4%, 0.9%, and 5.5%, respectively.

To sum up, both regional and global economic growth is expected to rebound strongly in 2021 after the severe pandemic-induced downturn in 2020. The development of safe and effective vaccines was a positive shock to the regional and global economies. Despite the advent of vaccines, however, the economic outlook for developing Asia and the world remains subject to a great deal of uncertainty since COVID-19 is likely to persist for some time.

---

[2] Developing Asia comprises the 46 developing member economies of the Asian Development Bank.

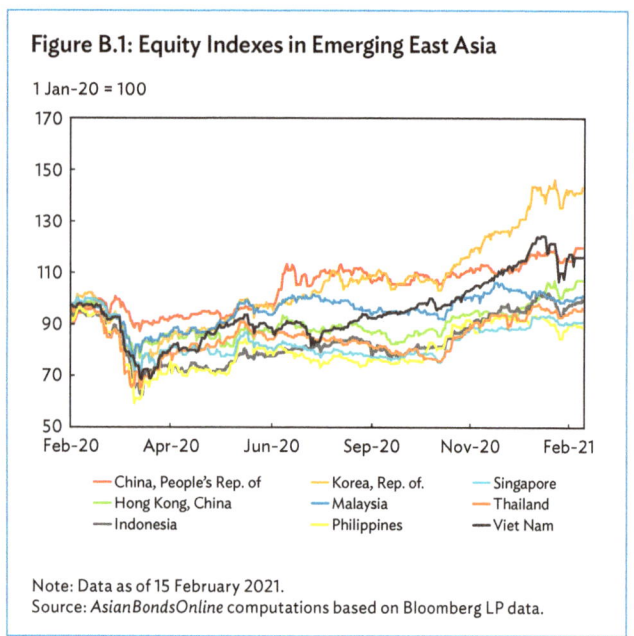

Figure B.1: Equity Indexes in Emerging East Asia

Note: Data as of 15 February 2021.
Source: AsianBondsOnline computations based on Bloomberg LP data.

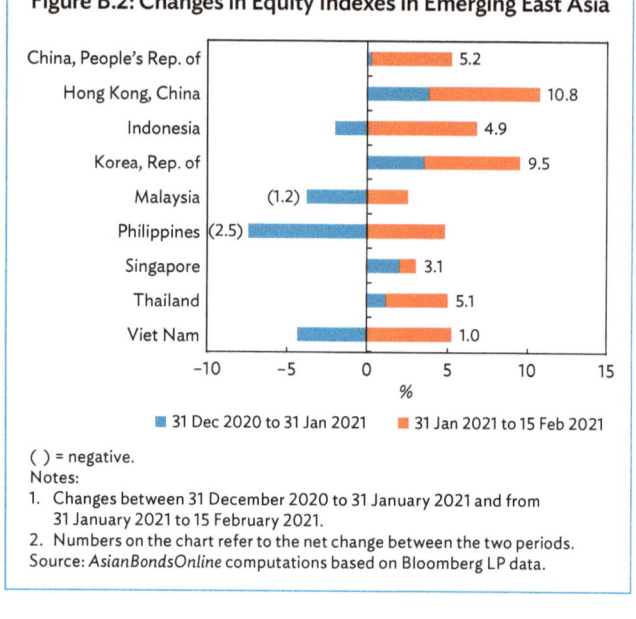

Figure B.2: Changes in Equity Indexes in Emerging East Asia

( ) = negative.
Notes:
1. Changes between 31 December 2020 to 31 January 2021 and from 31 January 2021 to 15 February 2021.
2. Numbers on the chart refer to the net change between the two periods.
Source: AsianBondsOnline computations based on Bloomberg LP data.

Improvement in investment sentiment supported regional equity markets. Most emerging East Asian economies posted equity gains during the review period (**Figure B.1**). Equity markets moved upward in the middle of February on progress on the proposed USD1.9 trillion stimulus package in the US (**Figure B.2**). The region's most rapidly rising equity market indexes were in Hong Kong, China and the Republic of Korea, which posted gains of 10.8% and 9.5%, respectively. The only exceptions to the regional trend were Malaysia (–1.2%) and the Philippines (–2.5%), with the latter posting the largest GDP decline among all markets in emerging East Asia in Q4 2020 at –8.3% y-o-y.

Positive investment sentiment was also seen in declines in risk premia, as credit default swap spreads largely trended downward (**Figure C**). Sovereign stripped spreads showed similar movements to the J. P. Morgan Emerging Market Bond Index Global (**Figure D**).

During the review period, regional currencies were broadly stable versus a weakened US dollar, with marginal movements (**Figure E.1**). The Chinese yuan strengthened the most, rising 1.1% from 31 December 2020 to 15 February 2021 on continued economic growth. The largest decline was in the Republic of Korea, where the won depreciated 1.4% versus the US dollar during the review period (**Figure E.2**).

The shares of foreign holdings in the region's bond markets posted mixed patterns in Q4 2020 (**Figure F**).

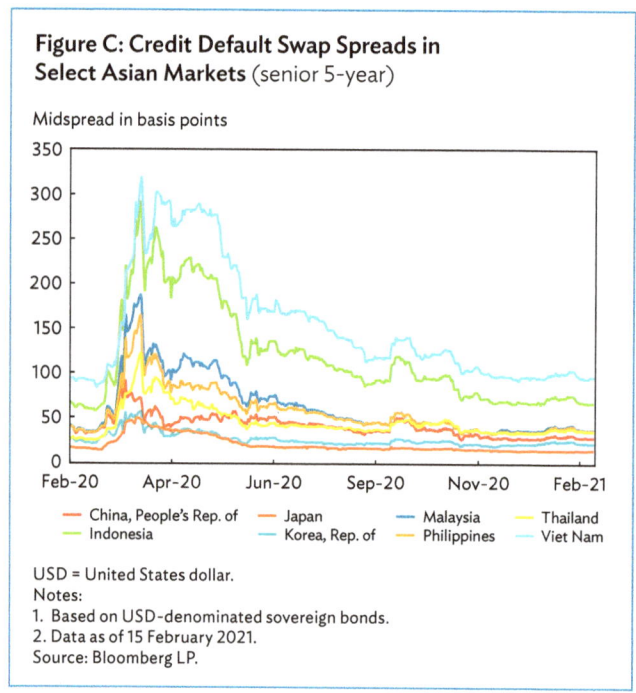

Figure C: Credit Default Swap Spreads in Select Asian Markets (senior 5-year)

USD = United States dollar.
Notes:
1. Based on USD-denominated sovereign bonds.
2. Data as of 15 February 2021.
Source: Bloomberg LP.

The share of foreign holdings in the PRC bond market gained 0.3 percentage points during the quarter. After declining throughout much of the year, the share of foreign holdings in the Philippines recovered to 2.7% at the end of December as investment sentiment improved. The foreign holdings share in Malaysia rose by 1.6 percentage points in Q4 2020 to reach 25.2% at the end of December. The foreign holdings shares in Thailand and Indonesia

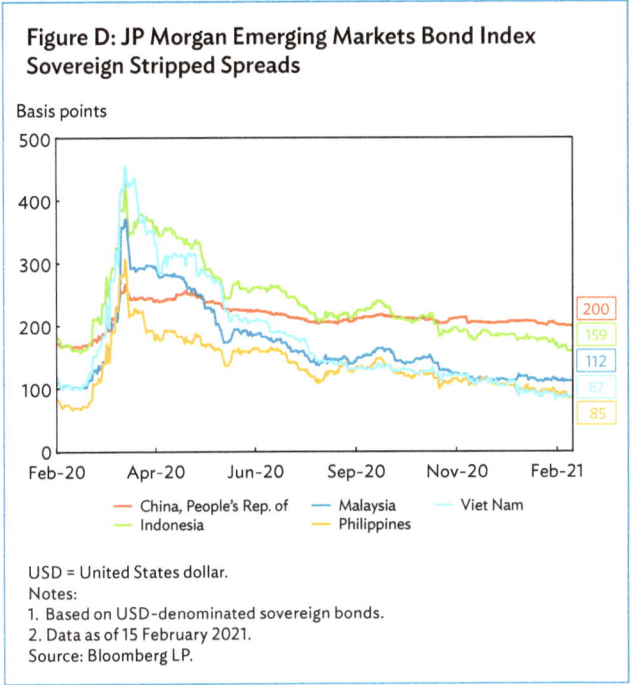

Figure D: JP Morgan Emerging Markets Bond Index Sovereign Stripped Spreads

USD = United States dollar.
Notes:
1. Based on USD-denominated sovereign bonds.
2. Data as of 15 February 2021.
Source: Bloomberg LP.

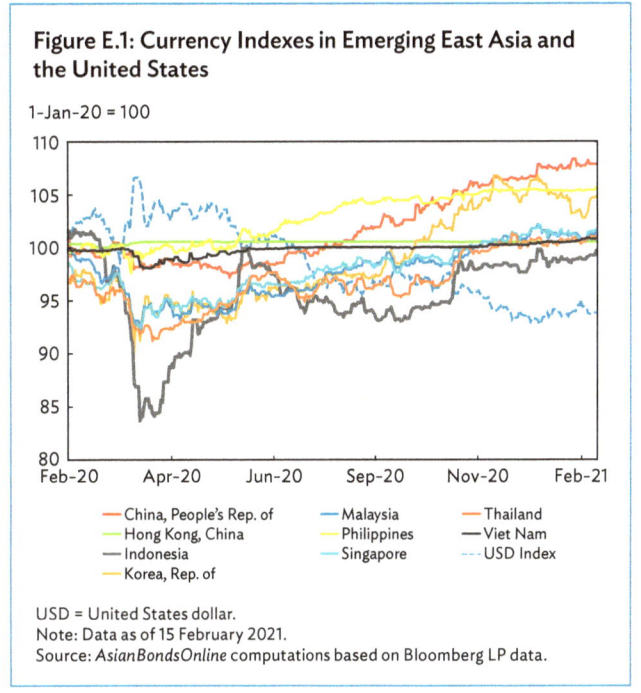

Figure E.1: Currency Indexes in Emerging East Asia and the United States

USD = United States dollar.
Note: Data as of 15 February 2021.
Source: *AsianBondsOnline* computations based on Bloomberg LP data.

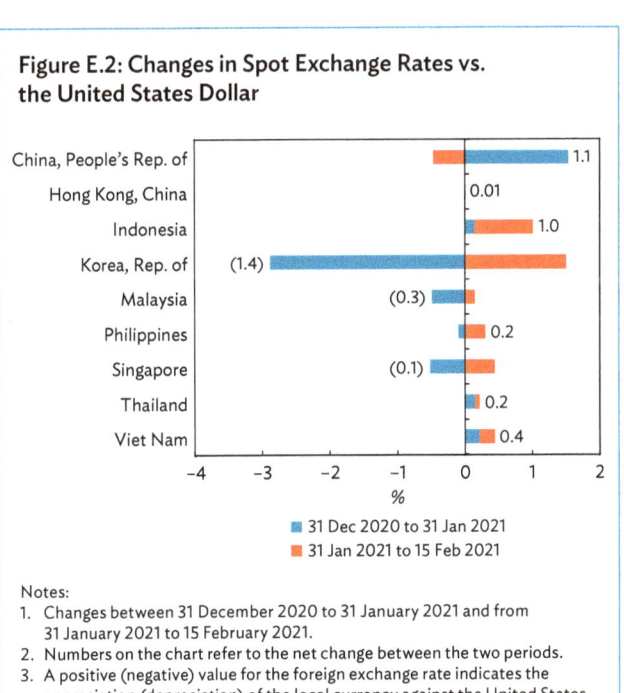

Figure E.2: Changes in Spot Exchange Rates vs. the United States Dollar

Notes:
1. Changes between 31 December 2020 to 31 January 2021 and from 31 January 2021 to 15 February 2021.
2. Numbers on the chart refer to the net change between the two periods.
3. A positive (negative) value for the foreign exchange rate indicates the appreciation (depreciation) of the local currency against the United States dollar.
Source: Bloomberg LP.

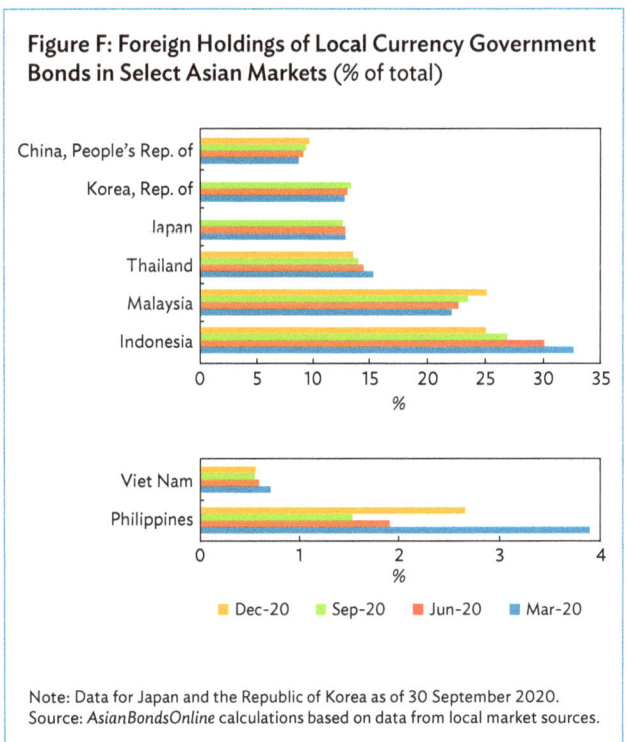

Figure F: Foreign Holdings of Local Currency Government Bonds in Select Asian Markets (% of total)

Note: Data for Japan and the Republic of Korea as of 30 September 2020.
Source: *AsianBondsOnline* calculations based on data from local market sources.

registered declines of 0.4 percentage points and 1.8 percentage points, respectively, in Q4 2020.

Risks to Economic Outlook and Financial Stability

Broadly speaking, the risk that COVID-19 poses to the world economy and financial markets has receded tangibly. The development of multiple safe and effective vaccines is a massive game-changer that can show a clear path toward the normalization of the economy and society. The unexpectedly rapid development of vaccines is nothing short of a miracle and a testament to the ingenuity and hard work of the medical and scientific communities. The experience of Israel, which leads the world in terms of vaccination rate, gives plenty of cause for optimism that vaccines will restore the world to pre-COVID-19 normalcy or something close to that. Infection rates are coming down sharply, social distancing restrictions are being relaxed, and the economy is being reopened.

Notwithstanding the arrival of safe and effective vaccines, the overarching risk to the global economic outlook and financial stability remains the trajectory of the COVID-19 pandemic. There are a number of reasons why vaccine development mitigates the risk from the pandemic but does not eliminate it altogether. In fact, while this risk has receded, it remains substantial for both emerging East Asia and the world.

Above all, vaccine rollouts have been uneven across countries. Specifically, most of the global supply of safe and effective vaccines has been secured by advanced economies. Some advanced economies such as Canada have secured quantities that are several times larger than their respective population. In stark contrast, many developing countries face a severe shortage of vaccines. Since COVID-19 is an infectious global disease that can easily cross borders, it will not be brought fully under control until much of the world, including developing countries, has been vaccinated. And as long as the virus is not contained across the world, there is a nonnegligible risk of a virulent resurgence like the one that ravaged Europe last fall. The slow progress of vaccine rollouts in developing countries thus harms the entire world.

There are negative factors that amplify the risk from the uneven vaccine rollouts and positive factors that mitigate the risk. On the negative side, the last few months have seen the emergence of new strains of COVID-19 in Brazil, South Africa, the United Kingdom, and elsewhere. There is some evidence indicating that particular variants may be more infectious and even more deadly. More importantly, there are concerns that existing vaccines may be less effective against some variants. These considerations make it all the more imperative for vaccines to be distributed and administered across the world before we see a proliferation of intractable variants.

On the positive side, the rapid rollout in advanced economies implies there will be more vaccines available for developing countries in the coming months. The COVID-19 Vaccines Global Access facility, which is commonly known as COVAX, has been set up by the World Health Organization and other bodies to promote equitable access to vaccines. The facility has already secured sizable supplies of vaccines for distribution to developing countries. Furthermore, some of the vaccines do not have to be stored at extremely cold temperatures, which reduces the storage and distribution logistics challenges for developing countries.

To sum up, the advent of safe and effective vaccines is a massive positive shock for the global economy and financial markets, but the world is not out of the COVID-19 woods yet. Far from it. The Israeli experience suggests that extensive vaccination can normalize the economy and society fairly quickly, even though the post-COVID-19 normal will differ in some ways from the pre-COVID-19 normal—e.g., voluntary social distancing and more work-from-home opportunities. Nevertheless, the slow progress of vaccine rollouts in many countries, especially developing countries, means that the threat of a virulent resurgence remains.

Beside risks that are directly related to COVID-19 and uneven vaccine rollouts, financial supervisory authorities would do well to monitor asset prices. Some of the abundant liquidity unleashed by global and regional central banks is finding its way into asset markets. In this connection, many stock markets around the world have risen sharply since the market volatility of early March 2020 (**Figure G**). While there are definitely major positive factors at play—such as vaccine development and the reopening of economies—it is not clear whether the magnitude of the escalation can be mostly, or even largely, explained by those factors. Potentially unsustainable asset price inflation fueled by monetary expansion entails the risk of a subsequent sharp and abrupt correction that could destabilize the financial system. Furthermore, the mix of monetary and fiscal stimulus may generate inflationary pressures for goods and services, not just assets. Central banks may respond by tightening monetary policy, which could destabilize financial markets. An additional source of potential risk is the passage of the USD1.9 trillion US fiscal stimulus program, which has triggered concerns about inflation, as evidenced by rising US bond yields. If the Federal Reserve responds by raising interest rates, the consequent tightening of global liquidity may cause a pullback of capital, which can potentially destabilize the region's financial markets.

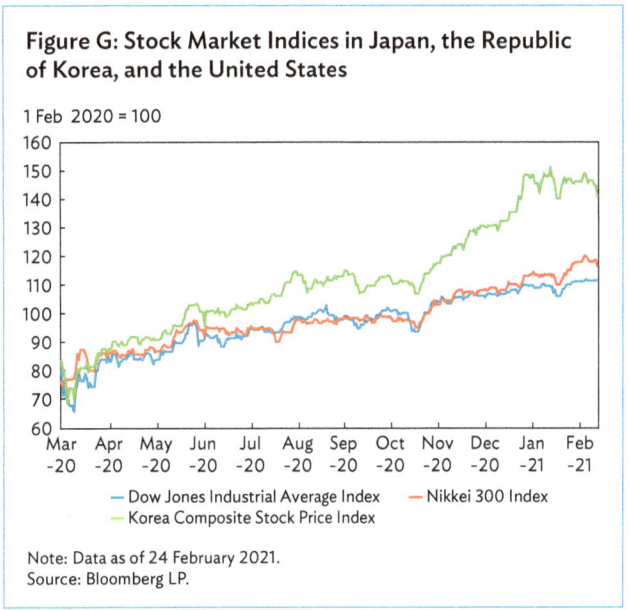

Figure G: Stock Market Indices in Japan, the Republic of Korea, and the United States

Note: Data as of 24 February 2021.
Source: Bloomberg LP.

Bond Market Developments in the Fourth Quarter of 2020

Size and Composition

The size of emerging East Asia's local currency bond market reached USD20.1 trillion at the end of December.

The outstanding amount of local currency (LCY) bonds in emerging East Asia reached USD20.1 trillion at the end of December.[3] Overall growth eased to 3.1% quarter-on-quarter (q-o-q) in the fourth quarter (Q4) of 2020 from 4.8% q-o-q in the third (Q3) quarter (**Figure 1a**). The slowdown in growth stemmed primarily from a contraction in issuance of government bonds in Q4 2020, as most governments had already met their financing needs to combat the impacts of the coronavirus disease (COVID-19) with large debt issuances in the previous quarters. Slower growth in the region's corporate bond market, driven mostly by a contraction in issuance amid lingering uncertainties over the trajectory of economic recovery, also curbed overall bond market growth during the review period. The q-o-q growth of bonds outstanding moderated in six of the region's nine markets between Q3 2020 and Q4 2020.

All markets except for Thailand posted positive q-o-q growth rates in Q4 2020. Among those that posted expansion, the region's smaller bond markets—Indonesia, Viet Nam, and the Philippines—recorded the fastest q-o-q expansion in Q4 2020, while the Republic of Korea, Malaysia, and the People's Republic of China (PRC) posted the weakest growth.

On a year-on-year (y-o-y) basis, emerging East Asia's LCY bond market growth quickened to 18.1% in Q4 2020 from 17.4% in the previous quarter (**Figure 1b**). All emerging East Asian bond markets except Thailand and the Republic of Korea saw a faster y-o-y expansion in Q4 2020 than in the preceding quarter. All nine markets in the region posted positive y-o-y growth in Q4 2020, with Viet Nam, the Philippines, Indonesia, and the PRC recording the fastest expansions.

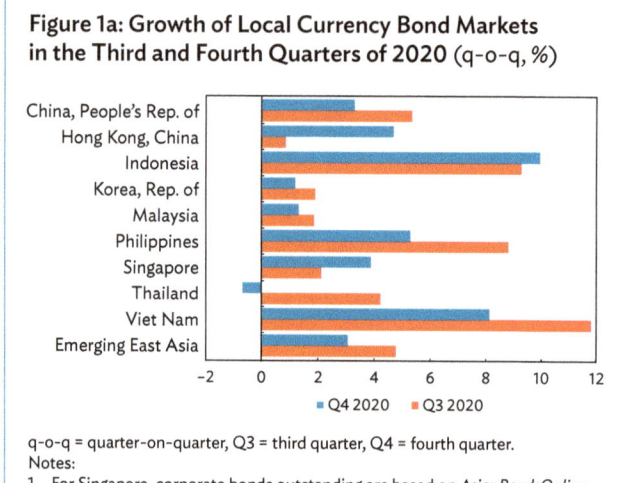

Figure 1a: Growth of Local Currency Bond Markets in the Third and Fourth Quarters of 2020 (q-o-q, %)

q-o-q = quarter-on-quarter, Q3 = third quarter, Q4 = fourth quarter.
Notes:
1. For Singapore, corporate bonds outstanding are based on *AsianBondsOnline* estimates.
2. Calculated using data from national sources.
3. Growth rates are calculated from local currency base and do not include currency effects.
4. Emerging East Asia growth figures are based on 31 December 2020 currency exchange rates and do not include currency effects.

Sources: People's Republic of China (CEIC); Hong Kong, China (Hong Kong Monetary Authority); Indonesia (Bank Indonesia; Directorate General of Budget Financing and Risk Management, Ministry of Finance; and Indonesia Stock Exchange); Republic of Korea (The Bank of Korea and KG Zeroin Corporation); Malaysia (Bank Negara Malaysia); Philippines (Bureau of the Treasury and Bloomberg LP); Singapore (Monetary Authority of Singapore, Singapore Government Securities, and Bloomberg LP); Thailand (Bank of Thailand); and Viet Nam (Bloomberg LP and Vietnam Bond Market Association).

The PRC remained the region's leader in terms of market size with its outstanding bond stock reaching USD15.5 trillion at the end of December. The PRC's share of emerging East Asia's total bond market inched up to 77.4% at the end of December from 77.2% at the end of September. Growth in the PRC's LCY bond market moderated to 3.3% q-o-q in Q4 2020 from 5.4% in Q3 2020. Both the government and corporate bond segments saw slower q-o-q growth in Q4 2020 than in the previous quarter. Growth in government bonds outstanding dropped to 3.8% q-o-q in Q4 2020 from 6.6% q-o-q in Q3 2020. A contraction in issuance of local government and policy bank bonds drove much of the growth slowdown in outstanding government bonds. Local governments completed most of their debt issuance in the previous quarters, resulting in a smaller issuance

---

[3] Emerging East Asia comprises the People's Republic of China; Hong Kong, China; Indonesia; the Republic of Korea; Malaysia; the Philippines; Singapore; Thailand; and Viet Nam.

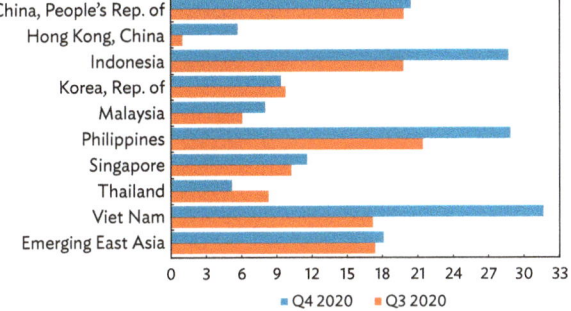

Figure 1b: Growth of Local Currency Bond Markets in the Third and Fourth Quarters of 2020 (y-o-y, %)

Q3 = third quarter, Q4 = fourth quarter, y-o-y = year-on-year.
Notes:
1. For Singapore, corporate bonds outstanding are based on *AsianBondsOnline* estimates.
2. Calculated using data from national sources.
3. Growth rates are calculated from local currency base and do not include currency effects.
4. Emerging East Asia growth figures are based on 31 December 2020 currency exchange rates and do not include currency effects.
Sources: People's Republic of China (CEIC); Hong Kong, China (Hong Kong Monetary Authority); Indonesia (Bank Indonesia; Directorate General of Budget Financing and Risk Management, Ministry of Finance; and Indonesia Stock Exchange); Republic of Korea (The Bank of Korea and KG Zeroin Corporation); Malaysia (Bank Negara Malaysia); Philippines (Bureau of the Treasury and Bloomberg LP); Singapore (Monetary Authority of Singapore, Singapore Government Securities, and Bloomberg LP); Thailand (Bank of Thailand); and Viet Nam (Bloomberg LP and Vietnam Bond Market Association).

volume in Q4 2020. Meanwhile, growth in the corporate bond segment eased from 3.2% q-o-q in Q3 2020 to 2.4% q-o-q in Q4 2020, driven largely by a drop in issuance amid several high-profile bond defaults during the review period. On an annual basis, growth in the PRC's LCY bond market rose to 20.5% y-o-y in Q4 2020 from 19.9% y-o-y in Q3 2020.

The Republic of Korea is home to the second-largest LCY bond market in emerging East Asia, with an outstanding bond stock of USD2.4 trillion at the end of December. Its share of the region's aggregate bond stock stood at 12.1% at the end of December. Growth in the Republic of Korea's total bond stock slipped to 1.2% q-o-q in Q4 2020 from 1.9% q-o-q in Q3 2020. The expansion in the aggregate LCY bond market was capped by weaker growth in the government segment, which outpaced the stronger growth in the corporate segment. Growth in outstanding government bonds dropped to 0.9% q-o-q in Q4 2020 from 3.0% q-o-q in Q3 2020, due mainly to a contraction in issuance. Meanwhile, growth in corporate bonds outstanding picked up, rising to 1.4% q-o-q in Q4 2020 from 1.1% q-o-q in the previous quarter. On a y-o-y basis, the Republic of Korea's LCY bond market growth eased to 9.4% in Q4 2020 from 9.8% in Q3 2020.

Hong Kong, China's LCY bond market reached a size of USD308.8 billion at the end of December, with growth jumping to 4.7% q-o-q in Q4 2020 from 0.9% q-o-q in Q3 2020. Hong Kong, China's bond market was one of the three bond markets in the region that posted faster q-o-q growth in Q4 2020 than in the preceding quarter. The faster growth stemmed from an accelerated expansion in both the government and corporate bond segments. Growth in the government bond segment soared to 2.3% q-o-q in Q4 2020 from 0.1% q-o-q in Q3 2020, driven primarily by a 30.1% q-o-q jump in the outstanding stock of Hong Kong Special Administrative Region (HKSAR) bonds. The expansion in HKSAR bonds was due to an unprecedented rise in issuance of HKSAR retail bonds, including HKD15.0 billion worth of 3-year inflation-linked bonds and HKD15.0 billion worth of 3-year Silver Bonds—a bond targeted at senior residents aged 65 and older. On the other hand, the stock of Exchange Fund Bills barely grew, while the stock of Exchange Fund Notes continued to contract due to limited issuance. Growth in corporate bonds accelerated to 7.1% q-o-q in Q4 2020 from 1.6% q-o-q in Q3 2020. On an annual basis, growth in Hong Kong, China's LCY bond market also quickened to 5.7% y-o-y in Q4 2020 from 1.0% y-o-y in the previous quarter.

At the end of December, the total amount of LCY bonds outstanding among member economies of the Association of Southeast Asian Nations (ASEAN) reached USD1,815.2 billion, up from USD1,755.5 billion (based on current exchange rates) at the end of September.[4] Overall growth moderated to 3.4% q-o-q in Q4 2020 from 4.7% q-o-q in Q3 2020. On a y-o-y basis, growth of aggregate ASEAN bonds outstanding accelerated to 13.9% in Q4 2020 from 11.4% in Q3 2020. The ASEAN member economies' share of the region's total bond stock was broadly steady at 9.0% between Q3 2020 and Q4 2020. The stock of government bonds amounted to USD1,297.7 billion at the end of December, accounting for a 71.5% share of the ASEAN total. Corporate bonds outstanding totaled USD517.5 billion and accounted for 28.5% of the aggregate ASEAN bond market. The LCY bond markets of Thailand, Malaysia, and Singapore remained the three largest in ASEAN at the end of December.

---

[4] LCY bond statistics for ASEAN include the markets of Indonesia, Malaysia, the Philippines, Singapore, Thailand, and Viet Nam.

The outstanding amount of LCY bonds in Thailand amounted to USD464.8 billion at the end of December. Thailand was the only bond market in the region that posted negative q-o-q growth in Q4 2020, due to contractions in both the government and corporate bond segments. The 0.3% q-o-q decline in government bonds outstanding in Q4 2020 was in contrast to the 5.4% expansion posted in Q3 2020. Similarly, the 1.8% q-o-q drop in corporate bonds in Q4 2020 reversed the 1.1% q-o-q growth recorded in the previous quarter. A high volume of maturities during the quarter brought about much of the decline in the outstanding stock of both government and corporate bonds. On a y-o-y basis, Thai LCY bond market growth slipped to 5.2% in Q4 2020 from 8.3% in Q3 2020.

In Malaysia, total LCY bonds outstanding reached USD399.1 billion at the end of December. Growth moderated to 1.3% q-o-q in Q4 2020 from 1.9% q-o-q in Q3 2020. The slowdown in growth stemmed largely from weaker growth in the government bond segment, where expansion eased to 0.5% q-o-q in Q4 2020 from 2.3% q-o-q in the previous quarter. Contractions in issuance of treasury and other government bonds, combined with a lack of new issuance and a relatively higher volume of maturities in central bank bills, brought about the slowdown in growth of government bonds outstanding. On the other hand, growth in corporate bonds rose to 2.2% q-o-q in Q4 2020 from 1.3% q-o-q in Q3 2020, buoyed by strong issuance. On an annual basis, growth in Malaysia's LCY bond market accelerated to 8.0% y-o-y in Q4 2020 from 6.1% y-o-y in Q3 2020.

Malaysia remained home to the largest *sukuk* (Islamic bond) market in emerging East Asia, with a total of USD252.8 billion in *sukuk* outstanding at the end of December. *Sukuk* accounted for 63.3% of the Malaysian LCY bond market. At the end of December, the outstanding stock of government *sukuk* totaled USD101.4 billion, or 47.8% of Malaysia's government bonds, while outstanding corporate *sukuk* reached USD151.4 billion, or 80.9% of the Malaysian corporate bond market.

Singapore's LCY bonds outstanding totaled USD380.4 billion at the end of December. Growth in total outstanding bonds rose to 3.9% q-o-q in Q4 2020 from 2.1% q-o-q in Q3 2020. Singapore was one of the three markets that recorded faster LCY bond market growth in Q4 2020 than in Q3 2020. The faster growth was driven primarily by the accelerated expansion of government bonds, with growth more than doubling to 5.3% q-o-q in Q4 2020 from 2.4% q-o-q in the previous quarter. Both Singapore Government Securities (SGS) bills and bonds and Monetary Authority of Singapore (MAS) bills contributed to the growth. On the other hand, growth in corporate bonds outstanding slowed to 1.3% q-o-q in Q4 2020 from 1.6% q-o-q in Q3 2020. On a y-o-y basis, Singapore's LCY bond market growth inched up to 11.6% in Q4 2020 from 10.2% in Q3 2020.

In Indonesia, the LCY bond market reached a size of USD321.5 billion at the end of December. Growth of total bonds outstanding quickened to 10.0% q-o-q in Q4 2020 from 9.3% q-o-q in Q3 2020. Indonesia posted the fastest q-o-q bond market growth in emerging East Asia in Q4 2020. The government bond segment drove the faster growth, as expansion of government bonds outstanding quickened to 11.6% q-o-q in Q4 2020 from 10.1% q-o-q in the previous quarter. The corporate bond segment recorded a 3.4% q-o-q decline in Q4 2020, reversing the 2.6% q-o-q rise in Q4 2020. A decline in issuance coupled with increased maturities resulted in a smaller outstanding stock of corporate bonds at the end of December. On a y-o-y basis, growth in Indonesia's LCY bond market soared to 28.7% in Q4 2020 from 19.8% in Q3 2020.

The Philippines' LCY bond market amounted to USD178.4 billion at the end of December. Overall growth slowed to 5.3% q-o-q in Q4 2020 from 8.8% q-o-q in Q3 2020. The slower growth was driven by a slowdown in the government bond segment combined with a contraction in the corporate bond segment. Growth in the outstanding stock of government bonds dropped to 7.0% q-o-q in Q4 2020 from 10.1% q-o-q in Q3 2020, primarily due to a contraction in issuance of treasury and government bonds; the government issued a fairly large amount of Retail Treasury Bonds in Q3 2020, which met most of its financing requirements to sustain the economy amid the pandemic. Due mainly to a high volume of maturities and lower issuances, the outstanding stock of corporate bonds contracted 1.3% q-o-q in Q4 2020. On a y-o-y basis, the Philippines' LCY bond market expanded 28.9% in Q4 2020, up from 21.5% in Q3 2020.

Viet Nam's LCY bond market remained the smallest in emerging East Asia with an outstanding bond stock of USD71.0 billion at the end of December. Overall bond market growth slowed to 8.1% q-o-q in Q4 2020 from

11.8% q-o-q in Q3 2020. Growth of government bonds outstanding eased to 7.1% q-o-q in Q4 2020 from 9.1% q-o-q in Q3 2020 due to weaker growth in the issuance of treasury and other government bonds. The expansion of the corporate bond market also slowed to 13.6% q-o-q in Q4 2020 from 28.0% q-o-q in Q3 2020 due to a deeper contraction in debt sales following a government decree that restricted corporate bond issuance. On a y-o-y basis, Viet Nam's bond market expanded 31.7% in Q4 2020, up from 17.2% in the previous quarter.

Government bonds continued to dominate emerging East Asia's LCY bond market in Q4 2020. The region's government bond stock reached USD12.4 trillion in nominal terms, representing a 61.8% share of the total LCY bond market at the end of December (**Table 1**). Except for Thailand, all government bond markets in the region posted positive q-o-q growth in Q4 2020. Nonetheless, growth in the region's government bond stock slowed to 3.6% q-o-q in Q4 2020 from 6.1% q-o-q in Q3 2020, amid weaker growth in most of the region's government bond markets. The q-o-q growth rate moderated in six out of the nine markets in the region in Q4 2020 versus Q3 2020, as most governments eased debt issuance after aggressively raising funds to combat the impacts of COVID-19 during the previous quarters. On a y-o-y basis, emerging East Asia's government bond stock expanded 19.5% in Q4 2020, up from 17.3% in Q3 2020.

The PRC and the Republic of Korea maintained their positions as the two largest government bond markets in the region with a combined share of 88.3% of the region's government bond stock at the end of December. ASEAN economies held 10.4% of the region's government bond total. Among ASEAN economies, the largest government bond markets were those of Thailand, Indonesia, and Singapore.

LCY corporate bonds outstanding in emerging East Asia stood at USD7.7 trillion at the end of December, accounting for a 38.2% share of the region's total LCY bond market. Growth in the region's aggregate corporate bonds outstanding slipped to 2.2% q-o-q in Q4 2020 from 2.7% q-o-q in Q3 2020. The slower growth was due mainly to a growth slowdown in six of the nine markets, including the region's two biggest markets, the PRC and the Republic of Korea. Nonetheless, all markets except for Indonesia, the Philippines, and Thailand saw positive q-o-q growth in corporate bonds outstanding in Q4 2020. On a y-o-y basis, growth in the region's LCY corporate bond stock dipped to 16.1% in Q4 2020 from 17.6% in the prior quarter. Meanwhile, a **Box** on page 13 compares the expansion of the corporate bond markets in East Asia and Latin America and its implications on financial resilience.

At the end of December, the corporate bond markets of the PRC and the Republic of Korea accounted for a combined 91.2% share of emerging East Asia's corporate bond stock, while the corporate bond markets of ASEAN member economies had a 6.8% share of the region's corporate bond total. Among ASEAN members, the largest corporate bond markets were in Malaysia, Singapore, and Thailand.

Emerging East Asia's total LCY bond market as a share of the region's gross domestic product (GDP) expanded to 97.7% at the end of December from 95.9% at the end of September and 83.5% at the end of December 2019 (**Table 2**). The GDP shares of both government and corporate bonds rose in Q4 2020 from the previous quarter.

The government bonds-to-GDP share climbed to 60.4% from 59.1% during the review period, while the corporate bonds-to-GDP share increased to 37.3% from 36.8%. The higher shares resulted from the still modest economic growth in the region while LCY bonds outstanding increased as governments continued to raise funds for fiscal stimulus and firms issued bonds to finance their operations amid the reopening of regional economies. Taking advantage of low interest rates also remained a factor for increased debt issuance in the market.

All emerging East Asian economies saw increases in their share of bonds-to-GDP between Q3 2020 and Q4 2020. The bond markets of the Republic of Korea, Malaysia, and Singapore exceeded a 100% share of their respective economy's GDP at the end of Q4 2020. The PRC nearly breached this level with a share of 99.8%. Meanwhile, Viet Nam had the region's smallest bonds-to-GDP share at the end of December at 26.1%.

By segment, Singapore had the largest government bonds-to-GDP share in the region at the end of December at 70.2%, while Viet Nam had the smallest at 21.6%. The Republic of Korea continued to have the largest corporate bonds-to-GDP share at 84.9%, while Indonesia had the smallest at 2.8%.

Table 1: Size and Composition of Local Currency Bond Markets

	Q4 2019		Q3 2020		Q4 2020		Growth Rate (LCY-base %)				Growth Rate (USD-base %)			
	Amount (USD billion)	% share	Amount (USD billion)	% share	Amount (USD billion)	% share	Q4 2019 q-o-q	Q4 2019 y-o-y	Q4 2020 q-o-q	Q4 2020 y-o-y	Q4 2019 q-o-q	Q4 2019 y-o-y	Q4 2020 q-o-q	Q4 2020 y-o-y
China, People's Rep. of														
Total	12,090	100.0	14,457	100.0	15,537	100.0	2.8	14.1	3.3	20.5	5.5	12.7	7.5	28.5
Government	7,753	64.1	9,240	63.9	9,978	64.2	2.0	12.7	3.8	20.6	4.7	11.4	8.0	28.7
Corporate	4,337	35.9	5,217	36.1	5,559	35.8	4.1	16.7	2.4	20.1	6.9	15.2	6.5	28.2
Hong Kong, China														
Total	291	100.0	295	100.0	309	100.0	0.1	1.8	4.7	5.7	0.7	2.4	4.7	6.2
Government	152	52.2	149	50.6	153	49.5	1.0	1.2	2.3	0.2	1.6	1.7	2.3	0.7
Corporate	139	47.8	146	49.4	156	50.5	(0.9)	2.6	7.1	11.6	(0.3)	3.1	7.1	12.2
Indonesia														
Total	253	100.0	276	100.0	322	100.0	2.3	14.2	10.0	28.7	4.8	18.6	16.5	27.1
Government	221	87.3	246	89.3	291	90.6	2.4	15.2	11.6	33.6	4.9	19.5	18.2	31.8
Corporate	32	12.7	30	10.7	30	9.4	1.7	8.1	(3.4)	(4.4)	4.1	12.2	2.3	(5.6)
Korea, Rep. of														
Total	2,083	100.0	2,224	100.0	2,424	100.0	1.6	7.6	1.2	9.4	5.1	3.4	9.0	16.3
Government	824	39.5	914	41.1	993	41.0	(0.2)	4.2	0.9	13.3	3.3	0.1	8.7	20.6
Corporate	1,259	60.5	1,310	58.9	1,430	59.0	2.7	9.9	1.4	6.8	6.3	5.6	9.2	13.6
Malaysia														
Total	363	100.0	381	100.0	399	100.0	(0.5)	6.0	1.3	8.0	1.8	7.1	4.7	9.9
Government	189	52.1	204	53.6	212	53.1	(1.6)	4.7	0.5	10.3	0.7	5.8	3.9	12.2
Corporate	174	47.9	177	46.4	187	46.9	0.7	7.6	2.2	5.6	3.1	8.7	5.7	7.4
Philippines														
Total	131	100.0	168	100.0	178	100.0	(0.8)	9.0	5.3	28.9	1.5	13.1	6.3	36.0
Government	101	77.4	134	79.9	145	81.2	(2.1)	7.5	7.0	35.3	0.2	11.5	8.0	42.7
Corporate	30	22.6	34	20.1	34	18.8	4.0	14.5	(1.3)	7.1	6.5	18.8	(0.4)	13.0
Singapore														
Total	335	100.0	355	100.0	380	100.0	2.6	13.1	3.9	11.6	5.4	14.6	7.3	13.6
Government	212	63.4	229	64.7	249	65.5	3.1	16.9	5.3	15.3	5.9	18.4	8.7	17.4
Corporate	123	36.6	125	35.3	131	34.5	1.7	7.1	1.3	5.1	4.5	8.5	4.7	7.0
Thailand														
Total	446	100.0	444	100.0	465	100.0	2.2	6.4	(0.7)	5.2	45.5	60.4	4.8	4.3
Government	318	71.4	325	73.2	342	73.5	2.5	5.2	(0.3)	8.3	40.8	53.0	5.2	7.3
Corporate	127	28.6	119	26.8	123	26.5	1.6	9.4	(1.8)	(2.5)	58.9	82.4	3.6	(3.3)
Viet Nam														
Total	54	100.0	65	100.0	71	100.0	(3.8)	4.4	8.1	31.7	(3.6)	4.4	8.5	32.1
Government	49	91.6	55	83.6	59	82.8	(3.9)	5.4	7.1	19.0	(3.7)	5.4	7.5	19.4
Corporate	5	8.4	11	16.4	12	17.2	(2.8)	(5.5)	13.6	169.5	(2.7)	(5.5)	14.0	170.4
Emerging East Asia														
Total	16,045	100.0	18,664	100.0	20,085	100.0	2.4	12.5	3.1	18.1	6.0	12.1	7.6	25.2
Government	9,819	61.2	11,496	61.6	12,422	61.8	1.7	11.4	3.6	19.5	5.3	11.3	8.1	26.5
Corporate	6,226	38.8	7,168	38.4	7,663	38.2	3.5	14.2	2.2	16.1	7.1	13.4	6.9	23.1
Japan														
Total	10,966	100.0	11,492	100.0	12,115	100.0	0.5	1.6	3.2	5.0	0.02	2.6	5.4	10.5
Government	10,180	92.8	10,664	92.8	11,250	92.9	0.4	1.2	3.3	5.1	(0.1)	2.2	5.5	10.5
Corporate	786	7.2	828	7.2	865	7.1	1.8	7.7	2.3	4.6	1.3	8.7	4.5	10.1

( ) = negative, LCY = local currency, q-o-q = quarter-on-quarter, Q3 = third quarter, Q4 = fourth quarter, USD = United States dollar, y-o-y = year-on-year.

Notes:
1. For Singapore, corporate bonds outstanding are based on *AsianBondsOnline* estimates.
2. Corporate bonds include issues by financial institutions.
3. Bloomberg LP end-of-period LCY–USD rates are used.
4. For LCY base, emerging East Asia growth figures are based on 31 December 2020 currency exchange rates and do not include currency effects.
5. Emerging East Asia comprises the People's Republic of China; Hong Kong, China; Indonesia; the Republic of Korea; Malaysia; the Philippines; Singapore; Thailand; and Viet Nam.
6. For Indonesia, data for government bonds include nontradable bonds.

Sources: People's Republic of China (CEIC); Hong Kong, China (Hong Kong Monetary Authority); Indonesia (Bank Indonesia; Directorate General of Budget Financing and Risk Management, Ministry of Finance; and Indonesia Stock Exchange); Republic of Korea (The Bank of Korea and KG Zeroin Corporation); Malaysia (Bank Negara Malaysia); Philippines (Bureau of the Treasury and Bloomberg LP); Singapore (Monetary Authority of Singapore, Singapore Government Securities, and Bloomberg LP); Thailand (Bank of Thailand); Viet Nam (Bloomberg LP and Vietnam Bond Market Association); and Japan (Japan Securities Dealers Association).

Box: A Comparison of the Expansion of Corporate Bond Markets in East Asia and Latin America

Following the global financial crisis, corporate debt steadily increased in East Asian and Latin American economies.[a,b] Between 2010 and 2019, the ratio of corporate debt to gross domestic product in the median economy increased from 119% to 144% in East Asia and from 34% to 42% in Latin America. An increase in bond issuances by firms accompanied this growth in corporate debt. In a new study, we show stylized facts on the boom in corporate debt in East Asia and Latin America, and discuss some of the main risks associated with this development (Abraham, Cortina, and Schmukler 2021).

Although firms in both East Asia and Latin America increased their bond issuances during the 2010–2019 period, there are important differences between the two regions. Bond financing in East Asia was conducted through domestic markets and in local currency. In turn, bond financing in Latin America was conducted through international markets and in foreign currency. In the median East Asian economy, 72% of the total amount of bonds raised per year—which includes both local and foreign currency issuances—was issued in local currency from 2010 to 2019. This represented an increase of 7 percentage points relative to the annual share of local currency bond issuance from 2000 to 2007. In contrast, the share of local currency bonds over the total bonds raised per year in the median Latin American economy was 33% in the 2010–2019 period. From 2000 to 2007, local currency bond issuances captured about 57% of the total capital raised in bond markets per year (**Figure B1**).

Firms borrowing in international markets are typically larger than those borrowing in domestic markets. Thus, the growth in bond market activity in East Asia comprised the participation of smaller issuing firms than in Latin America. In fact, the size of the median firm issuing bonds declined (increased) in East Asia (Latin America) as the use of domestic (international) markets expanded after the global financial crisis. In 2016, the median issuer firm in Latin America was about 10 times larger than in East Asia.

The cost of issuing bonds declined after the global financial crisis in both Latin America and East Asia, which is consistent with the notion that an expansion in the supply of bond financing by investors drove the rise in bond issuance by firms. From 2010 to 2019, East Asian and Latin American firms issued bonds at yields that were about 25% lower than in the 2000–2007 period. In East Asia, yields of local currency bonds declined more than yields of foreign currency bonds (26% vs. 22%, respectively). In contrast, in Latin America,

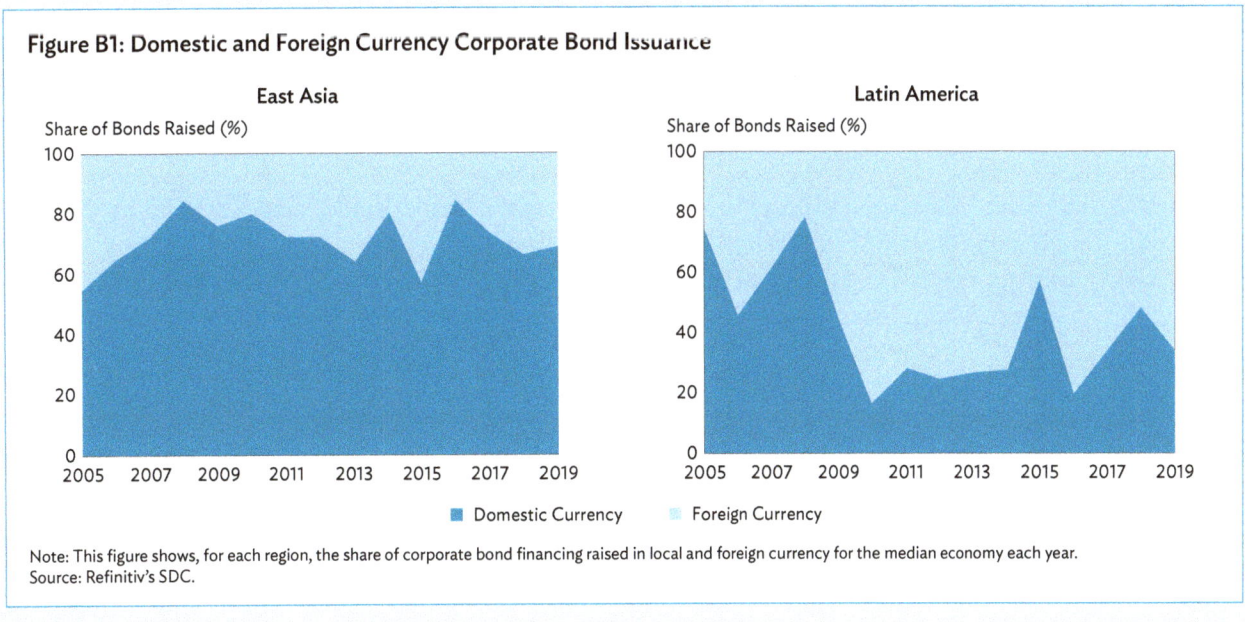

Figure B1: Domestic and Foreign Currency Corporate Bond Issuance

Note: This figure shows, for each region, the share of corporate bond financing raised in local and foreign currency for the median economy each year.
Source: Refinitiv's SDC.

---

[a] This discussion box was written by Facundo Abraham, Juan J. Cortina, and Sergio L. Schmukler of the Development Research Group of the World Bank. The box is based on F. Abraham, J. Cortina, and S. Schmukler. 2021. The Boom in Corporate Borrowing after the Global Financial Crisis: Different Tales from East Asia and Latin America. *World Bank Research and Policy Brief*. No. 42. World Bank Research and Development Center (Chile) and Malaysia Hub.
[b] East Asia includes the People's Republic of China; Hong Kong, China; Indonesia; the Republic of Korea; Malaysia; the Philippines; Singapore; Taipei,China; Thailand; and Viet Nam. Latin America includes Argentina, Brazil, Chile, Colombia, Costa Rica, Mexico, Panama, Peru, and Venezuela.

continued on next page

Box: A Comparison of the Expansion of Corporate Bond Markets in East Asia and Latin America *continued*

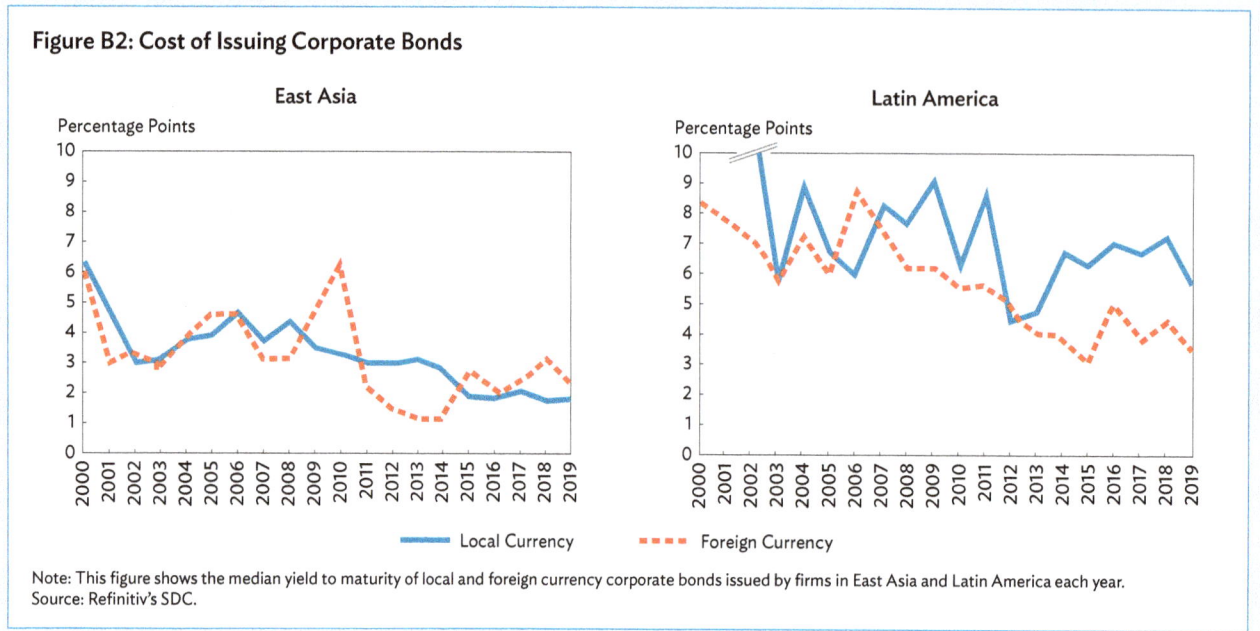

Figure B2: Cost of Issuing Corporate Bonds

Note: This figure shows the median yield to maturity of local and foreign currency corporate bonds issued by firms in East Asia and Latin America each year.
Source: Refinitiv's SDC.

yields of foreign currency bonds fell more than those of local currency bonds (30% vs. 23%, respectively) (**Figure B2**). As firms issued more bonds, their leverage positions rose and their financial performance worsened.

In the context of high debt accumulation, the economic and financial crisis triggered by the coronavirus disease (COVID-19) pandemic has heightened solvency risks in both regions. In East Asia, risks are related to the faster expansion in overall debt and to the fact that smaller firms, issuing bonds at shorter maturities, were behind the increase in bond issuance. In Latin America, firms are more vulnerable to changes in global market conditions than East Asian firms because they have relied more on foreign debt issued in foreign currency. Moreover, they have experienced larger currency depreciations than East Asian firms since the pandemic started.

Reference

Abraham, F., J.J. Cortina, and S.L. Schmukler. Forthcoming. The Expansion of Corporate Bond Markets in East Asia and Latin America. *Revue D' Economie Financiere, Debt and Developing Countries*.

Table 2: Size and Composition of Local Currency Bond Markets (% of GDP)

	Q4 2019	Q3 2020	Q4 2020
China, People's Rep. of			
Total	85.3	98.5	99.8
Government	54.7	63.0	64.1
Corporate	30.6	35.6	35.7
Hong Kong, China			
Total	79.1	83.4	88.3
Government	41.3	42.2	43.7
Corporate	37.8	41.2	44.6
Indonesia			
Total	22.2	26.5	29.3
Government	19.4	23.6	26.5
Corporate	2.8	2.8	2.8
Korea, Rep. of			
Total	130.2	141.6	143.8
Government	51.5	58.2	58.9
Corporate	78.7	83.4	84.9
Malaysia			
Total	104.5	116.9	119.6
Government	54.4	62.6	63.5
Corporate	50.1	54.3	56.0
Philippines			
Total	34.1	44.4	47.7
Government	26.3	35.5	38.7
Corporate	7.7	8.9	9.0
Singapore			
Total	88.2	101.5	107.2
Government	55.9	65.6	70.2
Corporate	32.3	35.9	37.0
Thailand			
Total	78.3	88.2	88.7
Government	55.9	64.5	65.2
Corporate	22.4	23.6	23.5
Viet Nam			
Total	20.6	24.5	26.1
Government	18.9	20.5	21.6
Corporate	1.7	4.0	4.5
Emerging East Asia			
Total	83.5	95.9	97.7
Government	51.1	59.1	60.4
Corporate	32.4	36.8	37.3
Japan			
Total	212.2	224.2	232.0
Government	197.0	208.0	215.5
Corporate	15.2	16.1	16.6

GDP = gross domestic product, Q3 = third quarter, Q4 = fourth quarter.
Notes:
1. Data for GDP are from CEIC.
2. For Singapore, corporate bonds outstanding are based on *AsianBondsOnline* estimates.

Sources: People's Republic of China (CEIC); Hong Kong, China (Hong Kong Monetary Authority); Indonesia (Bank Indonesia; Directorate General of Budget Financing and Risk Management, Ministry of Finance; and Indonesia Stock Exchange); Republic of Korea (The Bank of Korea and KG Zeroin Corporation); Malaysia (Bank Negara Malaysia); Philippines (Bureau of the Treasury and Bloomberg LP); Singapore (Monetary Authority of Singapore, Singapore Government Securities, and Bloomberg LP); Thailand (Bank of Thailand); Viet Nam (Bloomberg LP and Vietnam Bond Market Association); and Japan (Japan Securities Dealers Association).

Foreign Investor Holdings

Optimism prompted foreign investors to increase their holdings of LCY government bonds in Q4 2020 in most emerging East Asian markets.

Foreign holdings of LCY government bonds in emerging East Asia posted quarterly increases in Q4 2020 in all economies except for Indonesia and Thailand (**Figure 2**). The foreign investor shares are nearing, if not surpassing, the levels reached before the COVID-19 outbreak in the first quarter of 2020, which led to a massive sell-off in the region. Optimism over vaccines and a favorable economic recovery likely encouraged risk-on sentiment among foreign investors, leading them to scale up their participation in the region's debt market.

In the PRC, foreign holdings of government bonds climbed to 9.7% at the end of December, the highest level since data have been available. The growth in foreign ownership is a result of the rapid expansion of the LCY bond market accompanied by the continued integration of the PRC into global financial markets, which has made it easier to facilitate foreign fund entry. The PRC's sovereign debt also provides attractive returns on investments underpinned by the strong Chinese yuan and higher yields. A robust economic recovery from

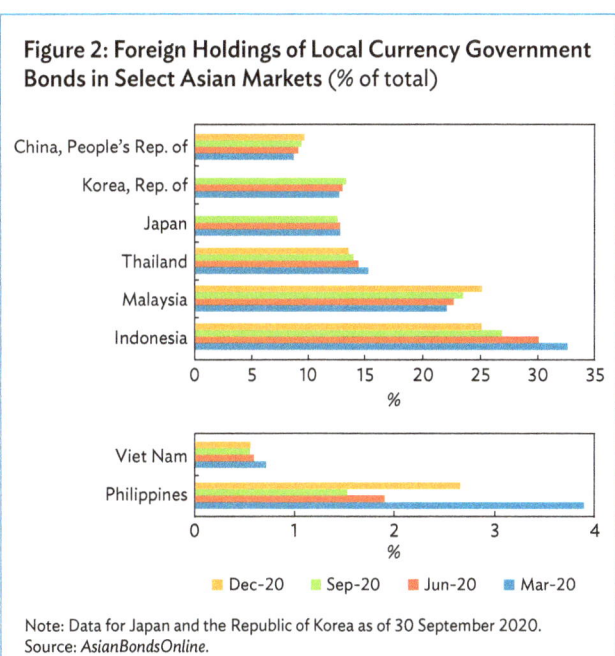

Figure 2: Foreign Holdings of Local Currency Government Bonds in Select Asian Markets (% of total)

Note: Data for Japan and the Republic of Korea as of 30 September 2020.
Source: *AsianBondsOnline*.

the impact of COVID-19 and the announcement by FTSE Russell that the PRC's government bonds would be included in the FTSE World Government Bond Index in October 2021 further piqued foreign investor interest.

Malaysia and the Philippines both experienced an increase in foreign holdings in Q4 2020. In Malaysia, foreign ownership of government bonds recovered to 25.2% at the end of December, up from 23.6% at the end of September and nearly reaching its pre-pandemic level of 25.3% in December 2019. Steady foreign appetite amid improving sentiment and higher yields lifted the foreign holdings share to match that of Indonesia, which once had the region's highest rate of foreign participation in the government bond market. In the Philippines, foreign investors' share of sovereign debt nearly doubled to 2.7% the end of December from 1.5% at the end of September, although this was still below its level before the COVID-19 outbreak.

In Viet Nam, the share of foreign holdings was barely changed at the end of December from the previous quarter at 0.6%. While Viet Nam has been one of the most successful countries in managing the COVID-19 pandemic and has experienced a solid economic recovery, foreign participation in its local government bond market is still far from pre-pandemic levels. One reason for the slow return of foreign interest is the small size of Viet Nam's bond market, which makes it an unappealing investment option for offshore investors.

The foreign ownership share of government bonds fell in both Indonesia and Thailand. In Indonesia, the share declined 1.8 percentage points in Q4 2020 from the previous quarter to 25.2% at the end of December and was down 13.4 percentage points from a year earlier. Although offshore investors seemed to have regained confidence in the Indonesian market as evidenced by the positive fund inflows in Q4 2020, foreign participation remained well below the pre-pandemic level of 39.0%. A large amount of the government debt issued is being absorbed by local investors including the central bank. In Thailand, subdued foreign fund inflows in Q4 2020 on the back of low investment returns translated into a decrease in the foreign holdings share to 13.6% at the end of December from 14.0% at the end of September.

In the Republic of Korea, the foreign holdings share increased to 13.3% at the end of September from 13.0% at the end of June. Like the PRC, foreign participation has increased even amid the pandemic, aided by prompt action to contain COVID-19 that hastened economic recovery, and sustained by higher returns and sound macro fundamentals.

Foreign Bond Flows

Foreign funds continued to flow into emerging East Asian markets in Q4 2020 on optimism over the economic recovery and progress in COVID-19 vaccine procurement.

All economies in the region recorded net inflows into their government bond markets in Q4 2020 except for the Republic of Korea (**Figure 3**). The region received total net inflows of USD39.5 billion, which was slightly reduced by net outflows of USD0.8 billion from the Republic of Korea's bond market. The amount of foreign funds that entered the region in Q4 2020 showed a strong recovery from what the region experienced in the first quarter of 2020 when investors panicked in the wake of the COVID-19 outbreak and sold off USD4.3 billion of emerging East Asian government debt.

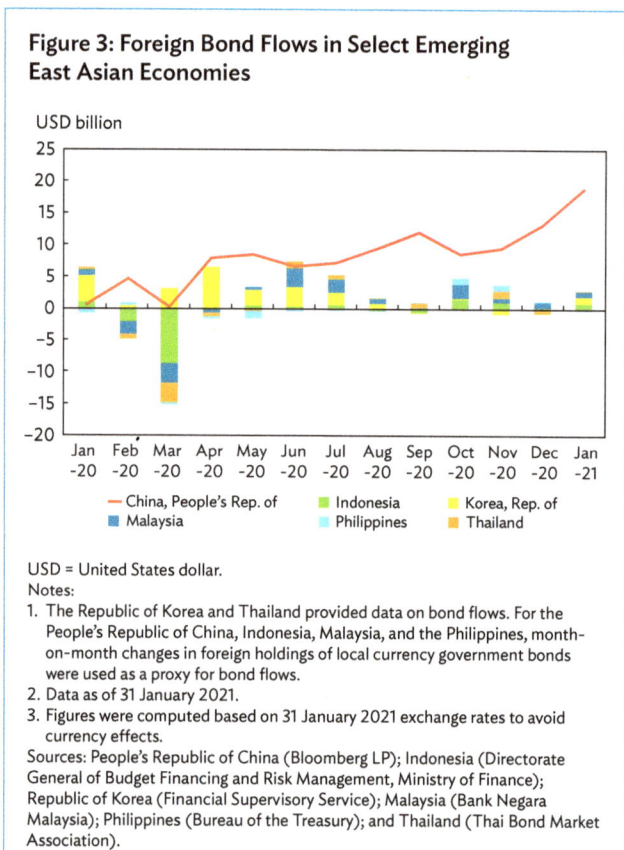

Figure 3: Foreign Bond Flows in Select Emerging East Asian Economies

USD = United States dollar.
Notes:
1. The Republic of Korea and Thailand provided data on bond flows. For the People's Republic of China, Indonesia, Malaysia, and the Philippines, month-on-month changes in foreign holdings of local currency government bonds were used as a proxy for bond flows.
2. Data as of 31 January 2021.
3. Figures were computed based on 31 January 2021 exchange rates to avoid currency effects.
Sources: People's Republic of China (Bloomberg LP); Indonesia (Directorate General of Budget Financing and Risk Management, Ministry of Finance); Republic of Korea (Financial Supervisory Service); Malaysia (Bank Negara Malaysia); Philippines (Bureau of the Treasury); and Thailand (Thai Bond Market Association).

The region's government bond market had a strong start in 2021, as it drew in USD21.5 billion of offshore funds in January, almost doubling the average monthly net inflows since its recovery began in April 2020. The sustained strong inflows were also a result of governments continuing to issue a considerable amount of debt to provide stimulus to the economy, while returns remained relatively higher in most markets in the region compared to advanced economies like the United States (US), making emerging East Asian assets attractive.

The PRC registered net inflows of USD31.3 billion in Q4 2020, the largest quarterly foreign buying in any quarter in 2020. In September, FTSE Russell announced it would include the PRC in its World Government Bond Index in October 2021. The PRC's entry into another major global bond index is expected to increase foreign participation in the LCY bond market. In January 2021, foreign investors purchased a net USD18.8 billion of PRC government debt, the highest monthly inflows since data are available, which indicates foreign investors are building their positions in the PRC's government bond market in the run-up to its inclusion in the FTSE Russell World Government Bond Index.

Malaysia and Indonesia were the largest recipients of foreign funds in the region after the PRC in Q4 2020. The inflows were underpinned by attractive yields and further boosted by low inflation, strong currencies, and improving sentiment over the economic recovery amid vaccination program rollouts.

In Malaysia, foreign investors bought a net USD3.7 billion of LCY government debt in Q4 2020. The impact of the sovereign ratings downgrade by Fitch Ratings in December was relatively muted, with inflows accelerating to USD0.9 billion in December from USD0.6 billion in November. The appetite for Malaysian government bonds remained sturdy through January, even with a spike of COVID-19 cases during the month, with net foreign buying amounting to USD0.9 billion. In Indonesia, inflows were at USD2.9 billion in Q4 2020, reversing net outflows of USD0.3 billion in the preceding quarter. In January, net foreign fund inflows registered USD1.0 billion.

The Philippines had net foreign fund inflows of USD1.9 billion in Q4 2020, reversing the USD0.3 billion outflow in Q3 2020 and marking the first quarterly net inflows since December 2018. The improvement is traced to the gradual reopening of the economy. While the Philippines registered inward fund flows of about USD1.0 billion each in October and November, net inflows dwindled in December to only USD36.9 million. In January 2021, foreign funds amounting to USD0.2 billion fled the government bond market amid uncertainty over the economic recovery given the detection of new COVID-19 variants and concerns over the arrival of vaccines.

Thailand had the smallest foreign fund inflows among the region's LCY government bonds markets in Q4 2020. Inflows amounted to only USD0.6 billion, down by more than half from USD1.5 billion in Q3 2020. Inflows in November were partly offset by outflows in October and December. In January 2021, Thailand registered very modest net inflows of USD3.9 million. Low returns on Thai government bonds, characterized by the small spread against US Treasuries, made them unattractive to foreign investors.

In contrast to other economies in the region, the Republic of Korea saw foreign funds retreat from its government bond market in Q4 2020, with outflows amounting to USD0.8 billion. Outflows were seen in November and December totaling USD1.0 billion, which offset the inflows in October. Most of the outflow was associated with the repatriation of funds from matured short-term securities as well as profit-taking toward the end of the year. In January 2021, the Republic of Korea's government debt market saw the reentry of foreign fund inflows of USD1.0 billion, which may be indicative of the reinvestment of proceeds.

LCY Bond Issuance

LCY bond issuance in Emerging East Asia reached USD2.0 trillion in Q4 2020.

LCY bond sales in emerging East Asia moderated to USD2.0 trillion in Q4 2020. On a q-o-q basis, bond issuance contracted 14.7% q-o-q following a 6.4% q-o-q expansion in Q3 2020 (**Table 3**). Due to a high base effect in the previous two quarters, issuance in Q4 2020 declined across all bond types except for central bank issuance, which recorded a slight uptick. Despite growth slowing down, gross issuance volume for the region was still higher than pre-COVID-19 levels, as the pandemic led to increased borrowing by governments and corporates. This highlights the importance of bond financing in capital raising for the needs of the public and private sectors.

Table 3: Local-Currency–Denominated Bond Issuance (gross)

	Q4 2019		Q3 2020		Q4 2020		Growth Rate (LCY-base %) Q4 2020		Growth Rate (USD-base %) Q4 2020	
	Amount (USD billion)	% share	Amount (USD billion)	% share	Amount (USD billion)	% share	q-o-q	y-o-y	q-o-q	y-o-y
China, People's Rep. of										
Total	834	100.0	1,574	100.0	1,294	100.0	(21.0)	45.5	(17.8)	55.2
Government	297	35.7	866	55.1	590	45.6	(34.5)	86.2	(31.8)	98.6
Central Bank	0	0.0	0	0.0	0	0.0	–	–	–	–
Treasury and Other Govt.	297	35.7	866	55.1	590	45.6	(34.5)	86.2	(31.8)	98.6
Corporate	536	64.3	707	44.9	703	54.4	(4.4)	22.9	(0.6)	31.1
Hong Kong, China										
Total	128	100.0	145	100.0	145	100.0	0.4	12.5	0.4	13.0
Government	109	85.2	117	80.8	112	76.9	(4.4)	1.6	(4.4)	2.1
Central Bank	109	84.6	117	80.7	107	73.7	(8.3)	(2.0)	(8.3)	(1.5)
Treasury and Other Govt.	1	0.6	0.1	0.1	5	3.2	3,550.0	461.5	3,548.5	464.3
Corporate	19	14.8	28	19.2	33	23.1	20.6	75.4	20.6	76.2
Indonesia										
Total	21	100.0	41	100.0	47	100.0	7.6	126.3	13.9	123.3
Government	19	88.3	39	93.9	46	96.8	10.8	147.9	17.3	144.7
Central Bank	8	39.2	9	21.6	14	29.7	47.7	71.5	56.4	69.3
Treasury and Other Govt.	10	49.2	30	72.3	32	67.1	(0.2)	208.7	5.7	204.7
Corporate	3	11.7	3	6.1	2	3.2	(42.5)	(37.1)	(39.1)	(37.9)
Korea, Rep. of										
Total	196	100.0	189	100.0	210	100.0	3.2	0.7	11.1	7.2
Government	60	30.5	85	44.8	78	37.2	(14.3)	23.0	(7.7)	30.8
Central Bank	29	14.6	31	16.2	29	13.8	(12.0)	(4.6)	(5.2)	1.5
Treasury and Other Govt.	31	15.9	54	28.6	49	23.4	(15.5)	48.3	(9.0)	57.8
Corporate	136	69.5	104	55.2	132	62.8	17.3	(9.0)	26.3	(3.2)
Malaysia										
Total	20	100.0	22	100.0	22	100.0	(0.3)	7.2	3.1	9.1
Government	9	43.5	12	57.4	8	35.1	(39.0)	(13.5)	(36.9)	(11.9)
Central Bank	3	14.6	0	0.0	0	0.0	–	(100.0)	–	(100.0)
Treasury and Other Govt.	6	28.9	12	57.4	8	35.1	(39.0)	30.2	(36.9)	32.5
Corporate	12	56.5	9	42.6	14	64.9	51.8	23.2	56.9	25.3
Philippines										
Total	7	100.0	25	100.0	29	100.0	13.2	268.5	14.3	288.7
Government	5	71.9	23	89.8	28	95.8	20.8	390.9	22.0	417.8
Central Bank	0	0.0	1	4.1	17	60.2	1,580.0	–	1,596.1	–
Treasury and Other Govt.	5	71.9	22	85.7	10	35.6	(53.0)	82.3	(52.5)	92.3
Corporate	2	28.1	3	10.2	1	4.2	(53.3)	(44.6)	(52.8)	(41.5)
Singapore										
Total	130	100.0	149	100.0	164	100.0	6.7	23.3	10.2	25.6
Government	128	98.4	145	97.5	160	97.9	7.2	22.7	10.7	25.0
Central Bank	103	79.3	119	80.2	135	82.5	9.8	28.2	13.4	30.5
Treasury and Other Govt.	25	19.1	26	17.3	25	15.5	(4.8)	0.0	(1.7)	1.8
Corporate	2	1.6	4	2.5	3	2.1	(12.0)	61.3	(9.1)	64.2
Thailand										
Total	79	100.0	93	100.0	74	100.0	(24.4)	(4.8)	(20.3)	(5.6)
Government	66	83.7	83	89.0	65	87.6	(25.6)	(0.4)	(21.5)	(1.2)
Central Bank	59	74.8	65	69.1	49	66.4	(27.4)	(15.4)	(23.4)	(16.1)
Treasury and Other Govt.	7	8.9	19	19.9	16	21.2	(19.4)	125.6	(15.0)	123.7
Corporate	13	16.3	10	11.0	9	12.4	(14.6)	(27.3)	(9.9)	(27.9)

continued on next page

Table 3 *continued*

	Q4 2019		Q3 2020		Q4 2020		Growth Rate (LCY-base %)		Growth Rate (USD-base %)	
	Amount (USD billion)	% share	Amount (USD billion)	% share	Amount (USD billion)	% share	Q4 2020		Q4 2020	
							q-o-q	y-o-y	q-o-q	y-o-y
Viet Nam										
Total	22	100.0	8	100.0	7	100.0	(6.8)	(66.5)	(6.4)	(66.4)
Government	22	99.2	5	63.7	5	73.3	7.3	(75.3)	7.7	(75.2)
Central Bank	20	88.5	0	0.0	0	0.0	–	(100.0)	–	(100.0)
Treasury and Other Govt.	2	10.8	5	63.7	5	73.3	7.3	128.2	7.7	129.0
Corporate	0.2	0.8	3	36.3	2	26.7	(31.6)	1,080.5	(31.3)	1,084.3
Emerging East Asia										
Total	1,439	100.0	2,246	100.0	1,993	100.0	(14.7)	32.0	(11.2)	38.6
Government	716	49.8	1,375	61.2	1,093	54.8	(23.5)	47.3	(20.5)	52.7
Central Bank	330	23.0	341	15.2	352	17.7	0.2	5.3	3.2	6.5
Treasury and Other Govt.	385	26.8	1,034	46.0	741	37.2	(31.3)	81.7	(28.4)	92.3
Corporate	723	50.2	871	38.8	901	45.2	(0.9)	17.3	3.4	24.6
Japan										
Total	418	100.0	533	100.0	771	100.0	41.6	75.2	44.6	84.3
Government	376	89.9	484	90.8	718	93.2	45.2	81.6	48.4	91.0
Central Bank	20	4.8	0	0.0	0	0.0	–	(100.0)	–	(100.0)
Treasury and Other Govt.	356	85.0	484	90.8	718	93.2	45.2	91.9	48.4	101.9
Corporate	42	10.1	49	9.2	53	6.8	5.4	18.0	7.7	24.1

( ) = negative, – = not applicable, LCY = local currency, q-o-q = quarter-on-quarter, Q3 = third quarter, Q4 = fourth quarter, USD = United States dollar, y-o-y = year-on-year.
Notes:
1. Corporate bonds include issues by financial institutions.
2. Bloomberg LP end-of-period LCY–USD rates are used.
3. For LCY base, emerging East Asia growth figures are based on 31 December 2020 currency exchange rates and do not include currency effects.
Sources: People's Republic of China (CEIC); Hong Kong, China (Hong Kong Monetary Authority); Indonesia (Bank Indonesia; Directorate General of Budget Financing and Risk Management, Ministry of Finance; and Indonesia Stock Exchange); Republic of Korea (The Bank of Korea and KG Zeroin Corporation); Malaysia (Bank Negara Malaysia); Philippines (Bureau of the Treasury and Bloomberg LP); Singapore (Singapore Government Securities and Bloomberg LP); Thailand (Bank of Thailand and ThaiBMA); Viet Nam (Bloomberg LP and Vietnam Bond Market Association); and Japan (Japan Securities Dealers Association).

Lower bond sales from the PRC dragged down the overall regional issuance volume during the quarter. Other regional markets that posted lower issuance activities in Q4 2020 versus Q3 2020 were Malaysia, Thailand, and Viet Nam. In contrast, quarterly issuance volumes rose in Hong Kong China; Indonesia; the Republic of Korea; the Philippines; and Singapore.

On a y-o-y basis, issuance volume climbed at a slower pace of 32.0% in Q4 2020 compared with a 39.9% expansion in Q3 2020. Nearly all emerging East Asian bond markets recorded positive y-o-y growth in bond issuance, with Thailand and Viet Nam as the exceptions. Both markets recorded y-o-y contractions during the review period. Growth on a y-o-y basis quickened in Hong Kong, China; Indonesia; Malaysia; the Philippines; and Singapore; while it moderated in the PRC and the Republic of Korea.

Government bonds accounted for 54.8% of the aggregate issuance volume during the quarter, declining from a 61.1% share in Q3 2020, largely due to the PRC's decline. Total LCY government bond issuance reached USD1,092.8 billion, with growth contracting 23.5% q-o-q but rising 47.3% y-o-y. Treasury instruments and other government bonds form the bulk of government bonds, representing a 67.8% share of the aggregate government bond issuance volume during the quarter in review. Growth declined 31.3% q-o-q in Q4 2020 but was up 81.7% y-o-y, as governments borrowed more in 2020 to fund pandemic stimulus programs. As in previous years, issuance volume slowed in the last quarter of the year as a majority of borrowing requirements have already been fulfilled earlier. On a y-o-y basis, all regional bond markets posted higher issuance growth for Treasury and other government bonds in Q4 2020 versus Q3 2020 except for the Republic of Korea, Malaysia, the Philippines, and Thailand. For Singapore, there was no change in the volume of issuance from the prior year.

On the other hand, issuance of central bank instruments inched up 0.2% q-o-q in Q4 2020, which was down from an 8.4% q-o-q uptick in the preceding quarter. Growth was fueled by increased issuance by Bank Indonesia, Bangko Sentral ng Pilipinas, and MAS. All other regional central banks tapered their issuance during the quarter versus that of Q3 2020, while Bank Negara Malaysia and the State Bank of Vietnam ceased issuance of central bank instruments.

Corporate bond issuance in regional markets contracted 0.9% q-o-q in Q4 2020, following a 0.6% q-o-q drop in Q3 2020. More active issuance from corporates in Hong Kong, China; the Republic of Korea; and Malaysia was observed during Q4 2020 versus Q3 2020. On the other hand, corporates from the PRC, Indonesia, the Philippines, Singapore, Thailand, and Viet Nam issued less. On a y-o-y basis, corporate bond issuance grew 17.3% in Q4 2020, slowing from a 24.2% rise in the earlier quarter.

The PRC was still the largest source of LCY bond issuance in emerging East Asia, albeit its share of the total fell to 64.9% in Q4 2020 from 70.0% in the prior quarter. Bond issuance volume in the PRC reached USD1,293.7 billion in Q4 2020 on a decline of 21.0% q-o-q after rising 6.9% q-o-q in Q3 2020. Both the q-o-q growth for government and corporate bonds contracted during the review period. The decline in government bonds was due largely to reduced issuance by local governments and policy banks. The quota for local government bond issuance had been mostly tapped by the end of Q3 2020, leading to less issuance for such bonds in Q4 2020. In addition, local governments were only given until October by the government to utilize the quota for the issuance of bonds under this program. On the other hand, issuance of Treasury instruments inched up 2.4% q-o-q during the review period. Issuance of corporate bonds fell 4.4% q-o-q after a marginal increase of 0.2% q-o-q in Q3 2020, amid cautious demand over corporate default rates and the possibility of increased oversight by government. Compared with the same period a year earlier, the PRC's issuance volume grew 45.5% y-oy in Q4 2020, down from 52.5% y-o-y in Q3 2020.

In the Republic of Korea, issuance activities were actively buoyed by the corporate bond segment. Total LCY bond issuance rose to USD210.2 billion in Q4 2020, with growth rebounding 3.2% q-o-q from a decline of 11.5% q-o-q in the prior quarter. Corporate bonds drove growth as issuance climbed 17.3% q-o-q, after posting declines in the previous 3 quarters. Growth in corporate bond issuance was buoyed by an improving economic outlook and corporates locking in low funding costs ahead of a projected rise in interest rates in 2021. In contrast, issuance of government bonds weakened by 14.3% q-o-q in Q4 2020. In terms of volume, however, issuance of government bonds remained higher than pre-COVID-19 levels and y-o-y growth in Q4 2020 remained at double-digit levels (23.0%). The government approved four supplementary budgets in 2020, necessitating the need for much higher issuance volume to support COVID-19 stimulus measures. On an annual basis, LCY bond issuance in the Republic of Korea grew 0.7% y-o-y in Q4 2020, down from 12.6% y-o-y in Q3 2020.

LCY bond sales in Hong Kong, China tallied USD145.2 billion in Q4 2020, with growth tapering to 0.4% q-o-q from 5.2% q-o-q in Q3 2020. Issuance of government bonds contracted 4.4% q-o-q, dragged down by a decline in the issuance of Exchange Fund Bills and Exchange Fund Notes. Issuance of Hong Kong Special Administrative Region bonds on the other hand surged in Q4 2020, buoyed by the issuance of 3-year iBonds and Silver Bonds in November and December. Corporate bond issuance was also more active, rising 20.6% q-o-q following an 8.2% q-o-q decline in Q3 2020. On a y-o-y basis, bond issuance growth quickened to 12.5% in Q4 2020 from 9.8% in the preceding quarter.

On an aggregate basis, LCY bond issuance by ASEAN economies reached USD344.2 billion in Q4 2020, representing a 17.3% share of emerging East Asia's issuance total during the quarter. Aggregate bond issuance in ASEAN markets slipped 2.2% q-o-q but rose 21.8% y-o-y in Q4 2020, compared with expansions of 17.8% q-o-q and 24.0% y-o-y in the preceding quarter. The markets of Indonesia, the Philippines, and Singapore posted increases in bond issuance volumes in Q4 2020, while Malaysia, Thailand, and Viet Nam pared their issuance volumes. The largest sources of LCY bond issuance among ASEAN members in Q4 2020 were Singapore, Thailand, and Indonesia.

Total LCY bonds sales from Singapore stood at USD163.8 billion during the quarter, with growth slipping to 6.7% q-o-q in Q4 2020 from 7.5% q-o-q in Q3 2020. Growth was driven solely by government bonds, particularly MAS instruments. On the other hand, issuance of SGS bills and bonds slowed during the quarter. Similarly, issuance of corporate bonds declined, falling

12.0% q-o-q in Q4 2020 on the back of a 16.1% q-o-q contraction in the earlier quarter. On a y-o-y basis, issuance volume increased 23.3% in Q4 2020 from 18.9% in Q3 2020.

In Thailand, LCY bond issuance summed to USD74.4 billion, with all bond types posting double-digit contractions in issuance during Q4 2020. Bond issuance declined 24.4% q-o-q in Q4 2020 after a 20.9% q-o-q hike in Q3 2020. The largest decline was seen in the issuance of central bank instruments, which slumped 27.4% q-o-q in Q4 2020 as the central bank boosted liquidity. Issuance of Treasury and other government bonds fell 19.4% q-o-q, while corporate bonds issuance declined 14.6% q-o-q. Some corporates held off their issuance plans, opting to borrow from banks due to lower borrowing costs. On an annual basis, bond issuance fell 4.8% y-o-y in Q4 2020 following growth of 23.4% y-o-y in Q3 2020.

LCY bond sales in Indonesia remained active through the fourth quarter, as the government continued to issue bonds to support its economy amid the COVID-19 outbreak. In past years, Indonesia normally cancels Treasury auctions by the middle of November, but its last auction for 2020 went into December. Total issuance in Q4 2020 tallied USD47.2 billion on growth of 7.6% q-o-q, down from a 44.0% q-o-q hike in Q3 2020. The volumes of issuance for Treasury bills and bonds were broadly at par with the issuance recorded in Q3 2020. In addition, Bank Indonesia issued more shari'ah-compliant central bank instruments during the quarter, as it implemented a number of changes to strengthen shari'ah monetary operations. In contrast, corporate bond issuance dropped 42.5% q-o-q in Q4 2020. On a y-o-y basis, bond issuance more than doubled in Q4 2020, with growth accelerating to 126.3% from 78.4% in Q3 2020.

In Malaysia, bond issuance in Q4 2020 stood at USD22.3 billion, broadly unchanged from its level in Q3 2020. Overall, growth was marginally down 0.3% q-o-q in Q4 2020 after declining 4.5% q-o-q in the preceding quarter. Similar with the Republic of Korea, the source of growth came from the corporate bond segment. During the quarter, issuance of government bonds dropped due to a decline in the issuance of Treasury instruments and the absence of issuance from Bank Negara Malaysia. On an annual basis, bond issuance inched up 7.2% y-o-y in Q4 2020 from 6.3% y-o-y in Q3 2020.

In the Philippines, total bond sales grew 13.2% q-o-q to USD29.1 billion in Q4 2020. Treasury and other government bond issuances declined 53.0% q-o-q as the government did most of its borrowing in earlier quarters. Corporate bond issuance also declined 53.3% q-o-q in Q4 2020 after soaring 358.3% q-o-q in the previous quarter. Q-o-q bond issuance growth was driven solely by central bank bonds, which rose more than 1,000% as the central bank sterilized foreign capital inflows. Q4 2020 bond issuance was still higher compared to pre-pandemic levels due to the need to fund stimulus measures. Bond issuance was higher by 268.5% y-o-y, driven mostly by a 390.9% y-o-y rise in government bonds.

In Viet Nam, total bond issuance declined 6.8% q-o-q in Q4 2020 to USD7.4 billion after rising 34.3% q-o-q in the prior quarter. While government bond issuance grew 7.3% q-o-q, overall issuance was dragged down by a 31.6% q-o-q decline in corporate bond issuance. Viet Nam's corporate bond issuance continued to be weak, as the government tightened corporate bond issuance standards in Q4 2020. On an annual basis, Viet Nam's bond issuance declined 66.5% y-o-y in Q4 2020 following a decline of 63.7% y-o-y in Q3 2020.

Cross-Border Bond Issuance

Emerging East Asia's cross-border bond issuance reached USD2.9 billion in Q4 2020.

Emerging East Asia's total intra-regional bond issuance reached USD2.9 billion in Q4 2020, a 53.9% q-o-q increase from the USD1.9 billion raised in the previous quarter. Institutions from five economies issued cross-border bonds in Q4 2020, led by firms from the PRC. Other economies that registered cross-border bond issuance in Q4 2020 include Hong Kong, China; the Republic of Korea; Malaysia; and Singapore. The first 2 months of the quarter saw a surge in issuance with total volumes of USD1.1 billion and USD1.4 billion in October and November, respectively. However, issuance dropped to USD394.8 million in December. From the same period in 2019, total intra-regional bond issuance increased 28.4%.

The PRC registered the highest aggregate issuance volume of USD2.4 billion in Q4 2020, dominating the market with a share of 81.7% (**Figure 4**). This was almost six times the USD400.8 million of issuance in Q3 2020 and a 70.2% y-o-y rise from Q4 2019. Banks and financial

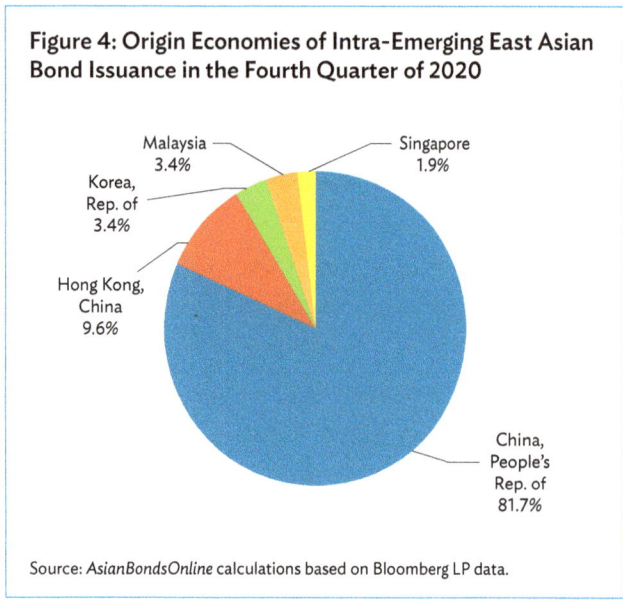

Figure 4: Origin Economies of Intra-Emerging East Asian Bond Issuance in the Fourth Quarter of 2020

Source: AsianBondsOnline calculations based on Bloomberg LP data.

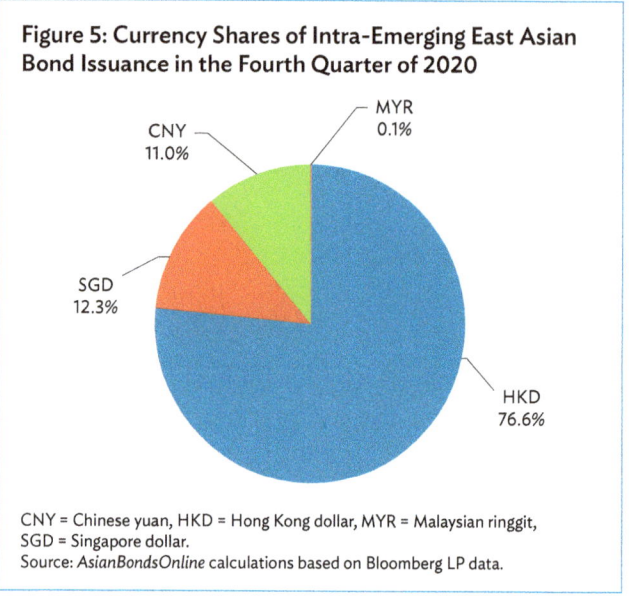

Figure 5: Currency Shares of Intra-Emerging East Asian Bond Issuance in the Fourth Quarter of 2020

CNY = Chinese yuan, HKD = Hong Kong dollar, MYR = Malaysian ringgit, SGD = Singapore dollar.
Source: AsianBondsOnline calculations based on Bloomberg LP data.

institutions accounted for over half of the total issuance in the PRC. A rise in the number of institutions that participated in cross-border bond issuance was also observed during the quarter, from only two in Q3 2020 to 14 in Q4 2020. Intra-regional bonds issued in the PRC were denominated in Hong Kong dollars, Malaysian ringgit, and Singapore dollars.

Institutions from Hong Kong, China issued a total of USD276.1 million, and all were denominated in Chinese yuan. This was a drop from the USD744.6 million raised in the previous quarter and almost at par with the issuance volume in the same period in 2019. State-owned Hong Kong Mortgage Corporation led all issuers with USD82.7 million worth of 1-year and 2-year bonds. Other notable cross-border issuances from Hong Kong, China include the USD82.0 million worth of 3-year bonds issued by HKCG Finance and the USD70.5 million multitranche bonds issued by KGI International Finance. State-owned railway company, MTR Corporation, also issued 3-year bonds worth USD30.6 million.

Cagamas Global, a state-owned mortgage corporation, was the sole issuer of intra-regional bonds in Malaysia, raising USD98.3 million worth of 1-year bonds denominated in Singapore dollars.

In the Republic of Korea, only two institutions issued intra-regional bonds in Q4 2020, with a total of USD98.1 million. Daewoo Engineering and Constructions issued USD56.7 million 3-year bonds issued in Singapore dollars, and the Export–Import Bank of Korea issued USD41.4 million worth of CNY-denominated 5-year bonds.

Among the five economies mentioned above, Singapore had the lowest cross-border issuance volume in Q4 2020 at USD56.2 million, led by CapitaLand Mall Trust MTN, which raised USD54.9 million worth of 10-year bonds denominated in Hong Kong dollars. Other institutions in Singapore that issued cross-border bonds in Q4 2020 include Nomura International Fund (USD0.8 million) and DBS Bank (USD0.5 million). Intra-regional bonds issued in Singapore were denominated in Chinese yuan and Hong Kong dollars.

The top 10 issuers of cross-borders bonds in Q4 2020 had an aggregate volume of USD2.4 billion and comprised 84.8% of the regional total; most issuances were denominated in Hong Kong dollars. Institutions from the PRC dominated the list, along with one firm each from Malaysia and Hong Kong, China.

The Hong Kong dollar continued to be the most widely used currency of intra-regional bonds in Q4 2020 with total volume of USD2.2 billion, comprising 76.6% of the regional total (**Figure 5**). Only firms from the PRC and Singapore had issuances in this currency during the quarter. The Singapore dollar followed with a share of 12.3% and a total of USD356.3 million issued by firms from the PRC, the Republic of Korea, and Malaysia. Other issuance currencies were the Chinese yuan (11.0%,

USD318.3 million) and the Malaysian ringgit (0.1%, USD2.6 million).

G3 Currency Issuance

Total G3 currency bond issuance in emerging East Asia amounted to USD378.1 billion in 2020.

The value of G3 currency bonds issued in emerging East Asia in 2020 totaled USD378.1 billion, expanding 9.1% y-o-y from USD346.6 billion in 2019 (**Table 4**).[5,6] The growth occurred despite a slight drop in the number of issuances in 2020 compared with 2019. The expansion was due to higher G3 issuance volumes in most of the region's economies compared with a year earlier. The COVID-19 pandemic and a low-interest-rate environment drove governments and companies to raise funds through G3 currency bonds.

Of all G3 currency bonds issued during the review period, a total of 91.9% was denominated in US dollars, 7.4% in euros, and 0.6% in Japanese yen. In 2020, a total of USD347.6 billion worth of bonds denominated in US dollars was issued in emerging East Asia, representing a jump of 9.8% y-o-y. The equivalent of USD28.2 billion of EUR-denominated bonds was issued during the review period, representing an increase of 26.6% y-o-y. Bonds issued in Japanese yen totaled USD2.4 billion, a decline of 69.5% y-o-y from a high base that was largely driven by Malaysia's samurai bond issuance in March 2019. In addition, most of the region's economies opted not to issue in Japanese yen during the review period.

The PRC continued to dominate the region's issuance of G3 currency bonds, totaling USD232.3 billion in 2020. This was followed by Hong Kong, China with USD34.8 billion and the Republic of Korea with USD30.0 billion. All three economies issued mainly in US dollars.

In 2020, G3 currency bond issuance increased on a y-o-y basis in the Philippines (129.6%); Singapore (52.1%); Malaysia (25.5%); Indonesia (24.5%); Hong Kong, China (9.1%); the PRC (3.1%); and the Republic of Korea (2.2%). Economies with decreased G3 currency bond issuance include Thailand (–18.4%) and Viet Nam (–91.8%). The Lao People's Democratic Republic had no issuance in 2020 while Cambodia issued G3 currency bonds during the review period after not issuing any in 2019.

The PRC accounted for 61.4% of all G3 currency issuance in emerging East Asia in 2020, issuing USD215.8 billion in US dollars and the equivalent of USD16.5 billion in euros. In Q4 2020, the PRC issued four tranches of USD-denominated bonds totaling USD6.0 billion and with tenors ranging from 3 years to 30 years. The issuance was significant as it was opened to US institutional investors. The PRC also issued EUR-denominated bonds with three tranches totaling USD4.9 billion and with tenors of 5 years to 15 years. Proceeds from the bonds will be used by the Ministry of Finance for general government purposes. Prosus raised USD1.5 billion from its 30-year bond issuance denominated in US dollars. The issuance came after the e-commerce company announced in October that it would buy back up to USD5.0 billion of its own shares and those of its parent company Naspers.

The Republic of Korea accounted for a 7.9% share of all G3 currency bonds issued during the review period: USD24.2 billion in US dollars and the equivalent of USD5.8 billion in euros. In Q4 2020, the Korea Development Bank issued a total of USD1.1 billion worth of USD-denominated bonds from various issuances with varying coupon rates and tenors ranging from 1 year to 6 years. The Export–Import Bank of Korea was also active during Q4 2020, issuing several bonds denominated in US dollars and totaling USD550.0 million. These included three 30-year callable zero-coupon bonds. The state-owned export credit agency of the Republic of Korea also issued a 2-year EUR-denominated bond worth USD51.3 million.

Hong Kong, China accounted for a 9.2% share of G3 currency bond issuance in 2020. By currency, USD33.2 billion was issued in US dollars, while EUR-denominated and JPY-denominated bonds amounted to USD1.0 billion and USD0.6 billion, respectively. In December 2020, the Airport Authority Hong Kong issued USD1.5 billion dual-tranche callable perpetual bonds denominated in US dollars. Proceeds from the issuance will be used for general corporate purposes, including the construction of a third runway. Conglomerate New World Development also issued a USD-denominated perpetual

---

[5] G3 currency bonds are denominated in either euros, Japanese yen, or US dollars.
[6] For the discussion on G3 currency issuance, emerging East Asia comprises Cambodia; the People's Republic of China; Hong Kong, China; Indonesia; the Republic of Korea; the Lao People's Democratic Republic; Malaysia; the Philippines; Singapore; Thailand; and Viet Nam.

Table 4: G3 Currency Bond Issuance

2019 Issuer	Amount (USD billion)	Issue Date	2020 Issuer	Amount (USD billion)	Issue Date
Cambodia	0.0		**Cambodia**	0.4	
China, People's Rep. of	225.2		**China, People's Rep. of**	232.3	
Tencent Holdings 3.975% 2029	3.0	11-Apr-19	Industrial and Commercial Bank of China 3.58% Perpetual	2.9	23-Sep-20
People's Republic of China (Sovereign) 0.125% 2026	2.2	12-Nov-19	Bank of China 3.60% Perpetual	2.8	4-Mar-20
People's Republic of China (Sovereign) 1.950% 2024	2.0	3-Dec-19	Bank of Communications 3.80% Perpetual	2.8	18-Nov-20
Others	218.0		Others	223.8	
Hong Kong, China	31.9		**Hong Kong, China**	34.8	
Celestial Miles 5.75% Perpetual	1.0	31-Jan-19	AIA Group 3.200% 2040	1.8	16-Sep-20
Hong Kong, China (Sovereign) 2.50% 2024	1.0	28-May-19	MTR Corporation 1.625% 2030	1.2	19-Aug-20
AIA Group 3.60% 2029	1.0	9-Apr-19	AIA Group 3.375% 2030	1.0	7-Apr-20
Others	28.9		Others	30.9	
Indonesia	22.4		**Indonesia**	27.9	
Perusahaan Penerbit SBSN *Sukuk* 4.45% 2029	1.3	20-Feb-19	Indonesia (Sovereign) 3.85% 2030	1.7	15-Apr-20
Indonesia (Sovereign) 1.40% 2031	1.1	30-Oct-19	Indonesia (Sovereign) 4.20% 2050	1.7	15-Apr-20
Indonesia (Sovereign) 3.70% 2049	1.0	30-Oct-19	Indonesia (Sovereign) 0.90% 2027	1.2	14-Jan-20
Others	19.0		Others	23.4	
Korea, Rep. of	29.4		**Korea, Rep. of**	30.0	
Republic of Korea (Sovereign) 2.500% 2029	1.0	19-Jun-19	Korea Housing Finance Corporation 0.010% 2025	1.2	5-Feb-20
Export–Import Bank of Korea 0.375% 2024	0.8	26-Mar-19	Korea Development Bank 1.250% 2025	1.0	3-Jun-20
LG Display 1.500% 2024	0.7	22-Aug-19	Export–Import Bank of Korea 0.829% 2025	0.9	27-Apr-20
Others	26.8		Others	26.9	
Lao People's Democratic Republic	0.2		**Lao People's Democratic Republic**	0.0	
Malaysia	13.7		**Malaysia**	17.2	
Malaysia (Sovereign) 0.530% 2029	1.8	15-Mar-19	Petronas Capital 4.55% 2050	2.8	21-Apr-20
Resorts World Las Vegas 4.625% 2029	1.0	16-Apr-19	Petronas Capital 3.50% 2030	2.3	21-Apr-20
Others	10.9		Others	12.2	
Philippines	6.7		**Philippines**	15.5	
Philippines (Sovereign) 3.750% 2029	1.5	14-Jan-19	Philippines (Sovereign) 2.65% 2045	1.5	10-Dec-20
Philippines (Sovereign) 0.875% 2027	0.8	17-May-19	Philippines (Sovereign) 2.95% 2045	1.4	5-May-20
Others	4.4		Others	12.6	
Singapore	9.7		**Singapore**	14.7	
DBS Group 2.85% 2022	0.8	16-Apr-19	United Overseas Bank 0.010% 2027	1.2	1-Dec-20
BOC Aviation 3.50% 2024	0.8	10-Apr-19	Oversea-Chinese Banking Corporation 1.832% 2030	1.0	10-Sep-20
Others	8.2		Others	12.5	
Thailand	6.4		**Thailand**	5.3	
Bangkok Bank in Hong Kong, China 3.733% 2034	1.2	25-Sep-19	Bangkok Bank in Hong Kong, China 5.0% Perpetual	0.8	23-Sep-20
Kasikornbank 3.343% 2031	0.8	2-Oct-19	PTT Treasury 3.7% 2070	0.7	16-Jul-20
Others	4.4		Others	3.8	
Viet Nam	1.0		**Viet Nam**	0.1	
Emerging East Asia Total	346.6		**Emerging East Asia Total**	378.1	
Memo Items:			**Memo Items:**		
India	21.9		India	14.3	
Indian Oil Corporation 4.75% 2024	0.9	16-Jan-19	Vedanta Holdings Mauritius II 13.00% 2023	1.4	21-Aug-20
Others	21.0		Others	12.9	
Sri Lanka	4.9		Sri Lanka	0.4	
Sri Lanka (Sovereign) 7.55% 2030	1.5	28-Jun-19	Sri Lanka (Sovereign) 6.57% 2021	0.1	30-Jul-20
Others	3.4		Others	0.3	

USD = United States dollar.
Notes:
1. Data exclude certificates of deposit.
2. G3 currency bonds are bonds denominated in either euros, Japanese yen, or US dollars.
3. Bloomberg LP end-of-period rates are used.
4. Emerging East Asia comprises Cambodia; the People's Republic of China; Hong Kong, China; Indonesia; the Republic of Korea; the Lao People's Democratic Republic; Malaysia; the Philippines; Singapore; Thailand; and Viet Nam.
5. Figures after the issuer name reflect the coupon rate and year of maturity of the bond.
Source: *AsianBondsOnline* calculations based on Bloomberg LP data.

bond worth USD700.0 million with a fixed coupon rate of 4.8%.

G3 currency bond issuance among ASEAN member economies increased 34.7% y-o-y to USD81.0 billion in 2020 from USD60.1 billion in 2019, as most ASEAN economies ramped up their issuance.[7] As a share of emerging East Asia's total G3 currency bond issuance in 2020, ASEAN issuance accounted for 21.4%, up from 17.3% in the previous year. Indonesia and Malaysia led all ASEAN members in terms of G3 currency bond issuance, followed by the Philippines, Singapore, Thailand, Cambodia, and Viet Nam.

Indonesia's G3 currency bond issuance in 2020 accounted for 7.4% of the total in emerging East Asia, comprising USD25.7 billion in US dollars, the equivalent of USD1.2 billion in euros, and the equivalent of USD1.0 billion in Japanese yen. Star Energy issued a dual-tranche USD-denominated green bond worth USD1.1 billion with tenors of 9 years and 18 years. Proceeds from the issuance will be used for the energy company's bond financing and geothermal operations. Indika Energy raised USD675.0 million from its 5-year callable bond denominated in US dollars. The integrated coal mining firm will use the proceeds to fund the redemption of some of its existing bonds.

G3 currency bonds issued by Malaysia accounted for 4.5% of emerging East Asia's total in 2020, including USD-denominated bonds worth USD16.6 billion and JPY-denominated bonds worth USD0.6 billion. During Q4 2020, Malayan Banking raised USD220.0 million from its issuance of 3-year and 40-year bonds, both denominated in US dollars. The short-term bond had a coupon rate of 0.882%, while the long-dated bond was a zero-coupon bond.

The Philippines accounted for 4.1% of total G3 currency bond issuance in emerging East Asia in 2020, comprising bonds denominated in US dollars and euros amounting to USD14.0 billion and USD1.5 billion, respectively. In December, the Philippines issued a USD-denominated dual-tranche bond worth USD2.8 billion with tenors of 10.5 years and 25 years. The proceeds from the global bonds will be used for the economy's general purposes including budgetary support. Power generation company SMC Global Power raised USD400.0 million from USD-denominated perpetual bonds for general corporate purposes, including the financing of liquefied natural gas facilities.

Singapore's share of G3 currency bond issuance in emerging East Asia was 3.9% in 2020, comprising USD12.9 billion in US dollars, the equivalent of USD1.7 billion in euros, and the equivalent of USD0.2 billion in Japanese yen. Temasek Financial was able to raise USD2.8 billion worth of USD-denominated bonds utilizing its global medium-term note program. The investment holding company issued a triple-tranche callable bond with tenors of 10 years, 30.5 years, and 50 years. United Overseas Bank also issued a long-dated bond with its 30-year callable, zero-coupon bond. The USD-denominated bond worth USD100.0 million was taken from the bank's debt issuance program.

During the review period, 1.4% of all G3 currency bonds issued in the region were from Thailand, comprising USD4.7 billion worth of bonds denominated in US dollars and USD0.5 billion in euros. Kasikornbank issued a USD500.0 million callable perpetual bond for general corporate purposes. During the same week as Kasikornbank's issuance, the Export–Import Bank of Thailand issued a USD350.0 million 5-year bond for general financing purposes.

In 2020, Cambodia issued USD0.4 billion worth of G3 currency bonds, contributing a 0.1% share of such bonds issued in the region during the review period.

Viet Nam accounted for 0.02% of all G3 currency issuance in emerging East Asia in 2020 with USD-denominated bonds worth USD80.0 million. Urban infrastructure developer Phu My Hung Development Corporation was the sole issuer in Viet Nam in 2020 with its 5-year, floating-rate note.

Figure 6 presents monthly G3 currency issuance in emerging East Asia from December 2019 to December 2020. G3 issuance declined in Q4 2020 as bond issuance activities from big issuers like the PRC, Indonesia, and the Republic of Korea declined during the quarter. Q4 2020, however, saw the issuance of numerous long-term tenors, with maturities ranging from 10 years to 50 years and some issues of perpetuals.

---

[7] ASEAN comprises Cambodia, Indonesia, the Lao People's Democratic Republic, Malaysia, the Philippines, Singapore, Thailand, and Viet Nam.

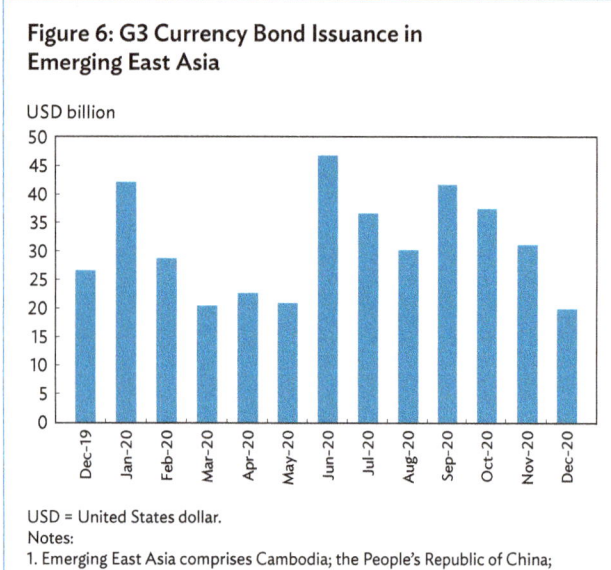

Figure 6: G3 Currency Bond Issuance in Emerging East Asia

USD = United States dollar.
Notes:
1. Emerging East Asia comprises Cambodia; the People's Republic of China; Hong Kong, China; Indonesia; the Republic of Korea; the Lao People's Democratic Republic; Malaysia; the Philippines; Singapore; Thailand; and Viet Nam.
2. G3 currency bonds are bonds denominated in either euros, Japanese yen, or US dollars.
3. Figures were computed based on 31 December 2020 currency exchange rates and do not include currency effects.
Source: AsianBondsOnline calculations based on Bloomberg LP data.

In 2020, Industrial and Commercial Bank of China issued the largest G3 currency bond with a USD2.9 billion perpetual USD-denominated bond issued in September. As the COVID-19 pandemic affected global financial markets, the March–May period saw the least G3 currency bond issuance in emerging East Asia. Issuances of G3 currency bonds picked up during the second half of 2020 as global financial market sentiment improved.

Government Bond Yield Curves

Local currency government bond yields rose at the longer-end of the curve for most emerging East Asian economies on the back of improved investor sentiment over the global economic recovery.

In Q4 2020, the outlook for the global economy largely improved as economies started easing quarantine measures and several drug makers released positive clinical trial results for their respective COVID-19 vaccines. The advent of the clinical trial results also allowed several economies to begin vaccination measures.

While there was some economic weakness in Q4 2020, central banks, particularly in advanced economies, noted that the weaknesses were expected to be transitory and the economic growth outlook was much improved, leading to an upgrade in economic forecasts.

In the US, economic growth tapered in Q4 2020, with GDP growing at annual rate of 4.1% versus 33.4% in Q3 2020. However, other economic data showed improvements with nonfarm payrolls improving in January, with additions of 166,000 following a decline of 306,000 in December 2020. In February, nonfarm payrolls further improved, increasing 379,000. The unemployment rate fell to 6.2% in February, from 6.3% and 6.7% in January and December, respectively. Retail sales also gained 7.6% month-on-month after falling 1.0% month-on-month in December.

In addition, the US Federal Reserve upgraded its economic projection in December from the previous September forecast, raising its 2021 GDP growth forecast to 4.2% from 4.0% and its 2022 forecast to 3.2% from 3.0%, The Federal Reserve also left its monetary policy unchanged during both its 15–16 December and 26–27 January meetings.

The European Central Bank (ECB), during its 10 December meeting, left its key policy rates unchanged but raised its pandemic emergency monthly purchase program by EUR500 billion to EUR1,850 billion and extended the duration to March 2022 from June 2021. The euro area's GDP declined 4.9% y-o-y in Q4 2020 after a decline of 4.2% y-o-y in Q3 2020. Unlike the US, the ECB downgraded its GDP forecasts in December from those in September. The 2021 GDP growth forecast was adjusted to 3.9% in 2021 from 5.0%. The 2022 GDP forecast was adjusted to 4.2% from 3.2%. However, the ECB said that it is somewhat optimistic that the medium-term outlook would improve over the ongoing vaccination programs in the region.

The Bank of Japan largely left monetary policy unchanged during its 17 December meeting but adjusted the duration of its purchase program for commercial paper and corporate bonds by 6 months to the end of September 2021. Japan also had positive annualized GDP growth in Q4 2020 of 11.7% after a 22.8% gain in the third quarter. Likewise, the Bank of Japan upgraded the 2021 GDP forecast to 3.9% in from 3.6% and the 2022 forecast to 1.8% from 1.6%.

The improving outlook for the global economy also pushed yields upward in emerging East Asia between

31 December and 15 February. For the 2-year maturities, yields rose for most economies in emerging East Asia with the exception of the Republic of Korea (**Figure 7a**). The steepest increase in the 2-year yield was in Indonesia (**Figure 7b**). After consistent declines for most of 2020, the 2-year yields spiked in Indonesia at the start of 2021.

In the same period, 10-year yields also showed a similar pattern, but with much steeper increases for most emerging East Asian markets. Unlike its 2-year yield, the Republic of Korea's 10-year yield trended upward (**Figure 8a**). While Indonesia's 10-year yield rose, the gain was not as steep compared to the 2-year yield (**Figure 8b**). Viet Nam was the sole exception to the rise in 10-year yields, as it trended downward on strong market demand.

The improved economic outlook also led to a steepening of yield curves in emerging East Asia between 31 December and 15 February (**Figure 9**). Yields shifted upwards for all tenors in Hong Kong, China and Thailand, and for all but a few tenors in the PRC, Indonesia, and Malaysia. In some economies, there were declines in shorter-term yields but a rise in longer-term yields. This

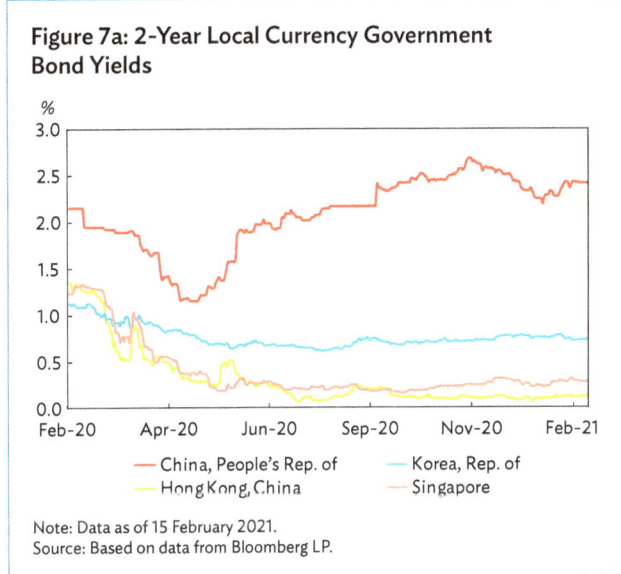

Figure 7a: 2-Year Local Currency Government Bond Yields

Note: Data as of 15 February 2021.
Source: Based on data from Bloomberg LP.

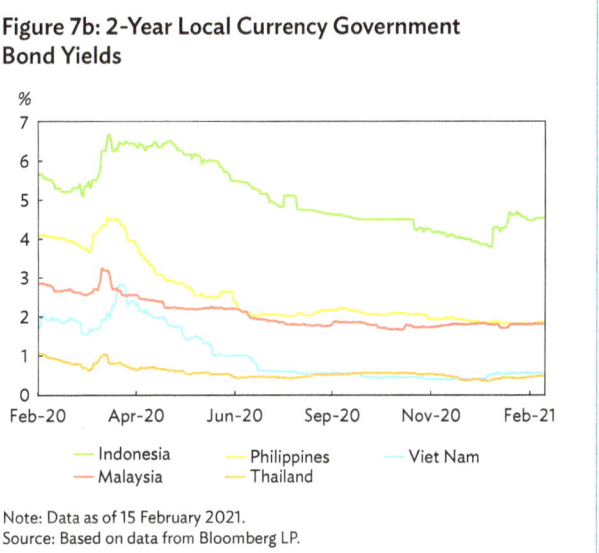

Figure 7b: 2-Year Local Currency Government Bond Yields

Note: Data as of 15 February 2021.
Source: Based on data from Bloomberg LP.

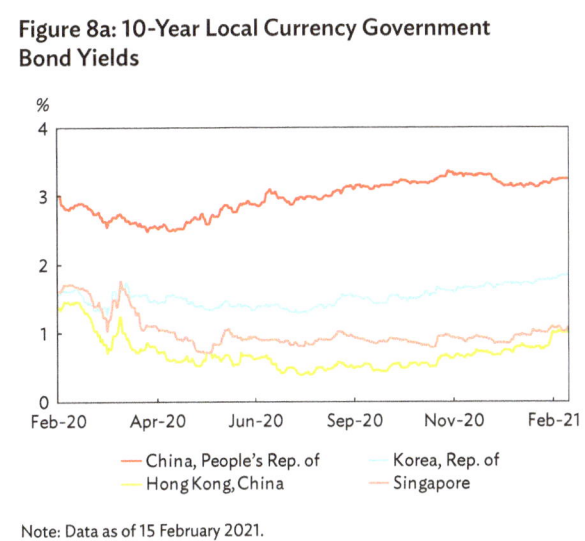

Figure 8a: 10-Year Local Currency Government Bond Yields

Note: Data as of 15 February 2021.
Source: Based on data from Bloomberg LP.

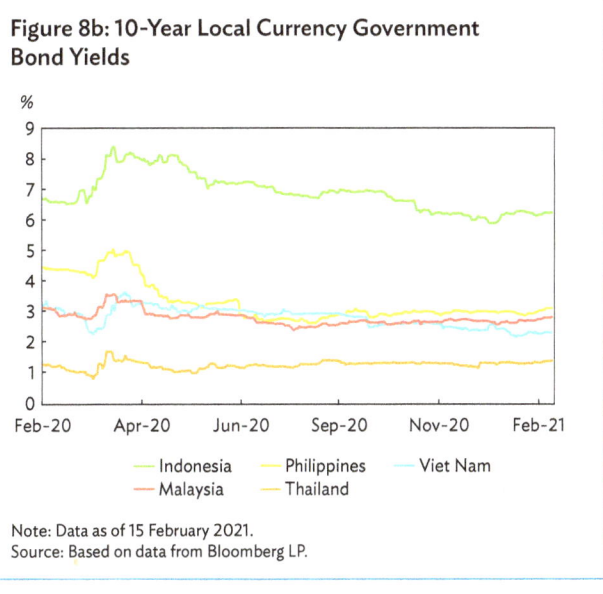

Figure 8b: 10-Year Local Currency Government Bond Yields

Note: Data as of 15 February 2021.
Source: Based on data from Bloomberg LP.

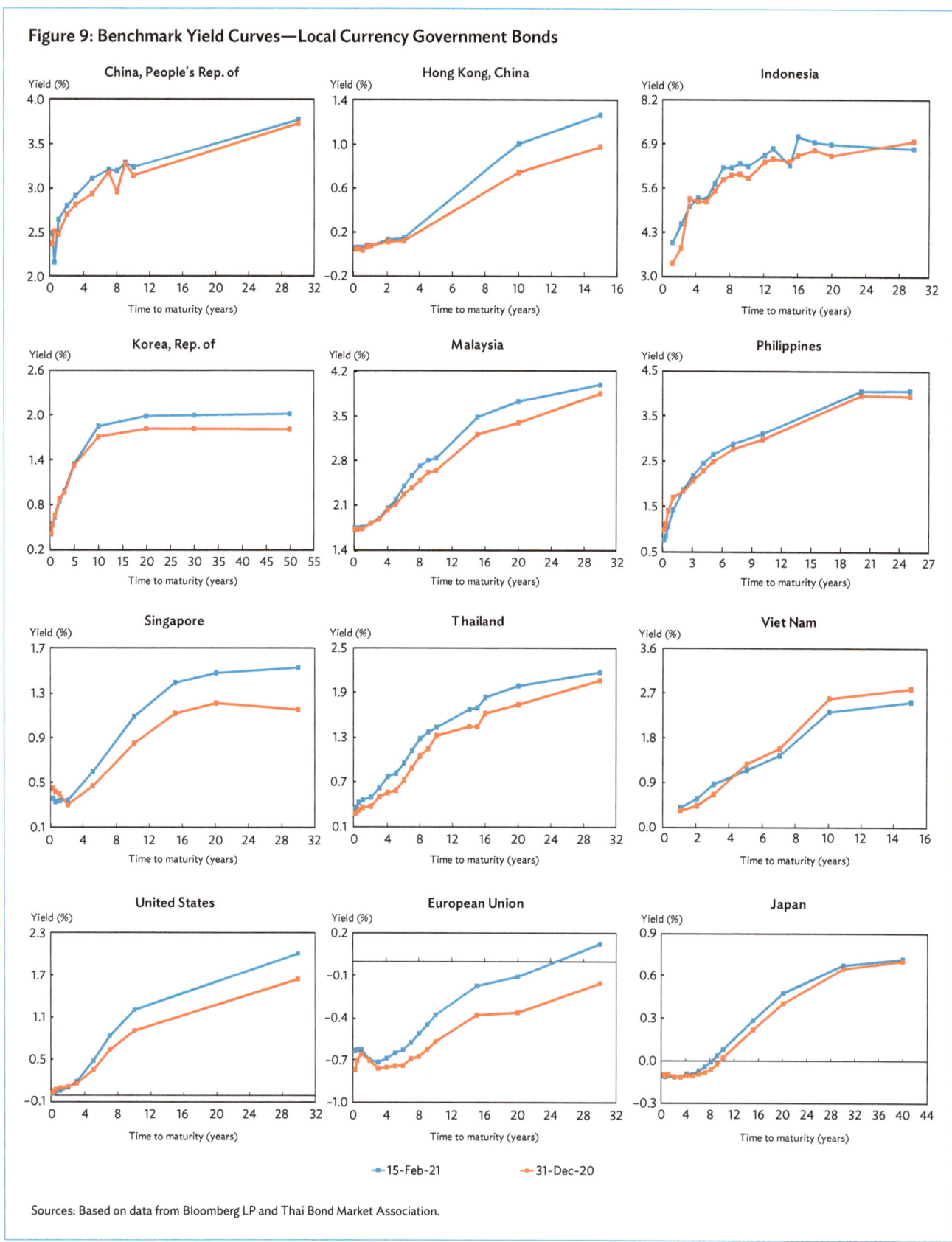

Figure 9: Benchmark Yield Curves—Local Currency Government Bonds

Sources: Based on data from Bloomberg LP and Thai Bond Market Association.

was the case in the Republic of Korea, the Philippines, and Singapore. Only Viet Nam was the exception, as its yield curve shifted upward at the shorter-end but downward at the longer-end. Rising global inflationary concerns due to past stimulus measures, however, may place further pressure on yields.

The 2-year versus 10-year yield spread widened for nearly all markets during the review period except in the PRC, where it was unchanged, and in Indonesia, Thailand, and Viet Nam, where it narrowed (**Figure 10**).

Nearly all emerging East Asian economies posted negative y-o-y growth rates in Q4 2020. The two exceptions were the PRC, which posted its third straight quarter of positive GDP growth, and Viet Nam, which had positive quarterly GDP growth rates throughout 2020. While the remaining markets posted negative y-o-y GDP growth rates in Q4 2020, consistent with the improving economic outlook and easing of quarantine measures, GDP mostly declined at a smaller y-o-y pace compared to the previous quarter. The exceptions were the Republic of Korea, which posted a 1.4% y-o-y decline in Q4 2020 after a 1.1% y-o-y decline in Q3 2020, and Malaysia, which posted a 3.4% y-o-y decline following a 2.6% y-o-y decline in the same period.

Inflation rates continued to be subdued in emerging East Asia in 2020 due to the economic downturn, with a number of economies having negative inflation rates. Despite positive economic growth, Viet Nam slipped into deflation in January with an inflation rate of –1.0% (**Figure 11a**). Indonesia's inflation rate continues to be stable, alongside the inflation rate of the Republic

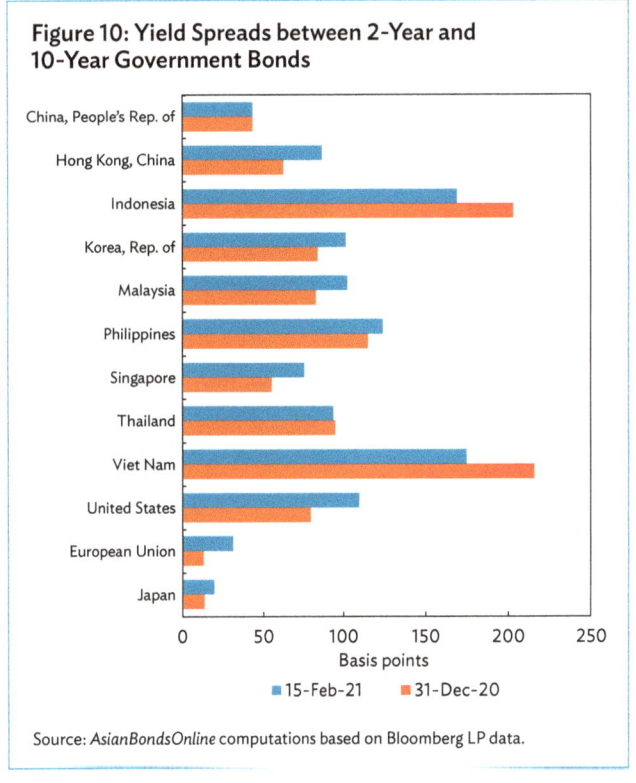

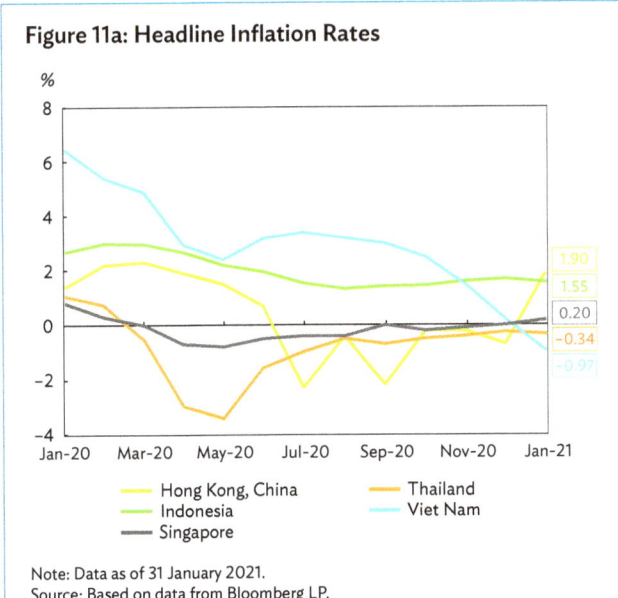

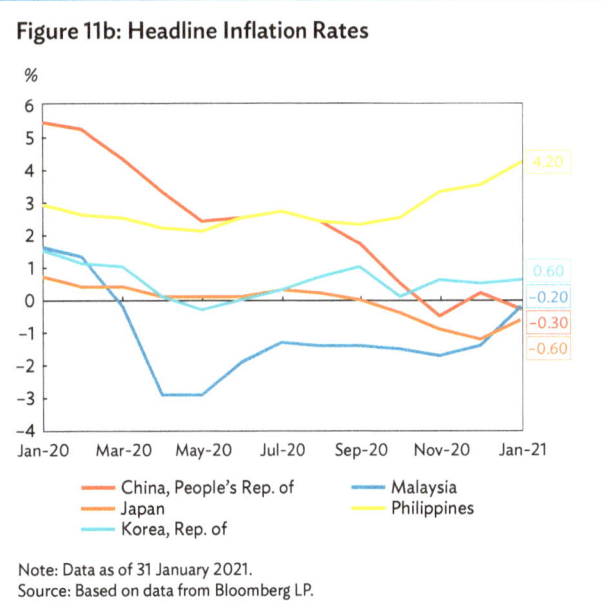

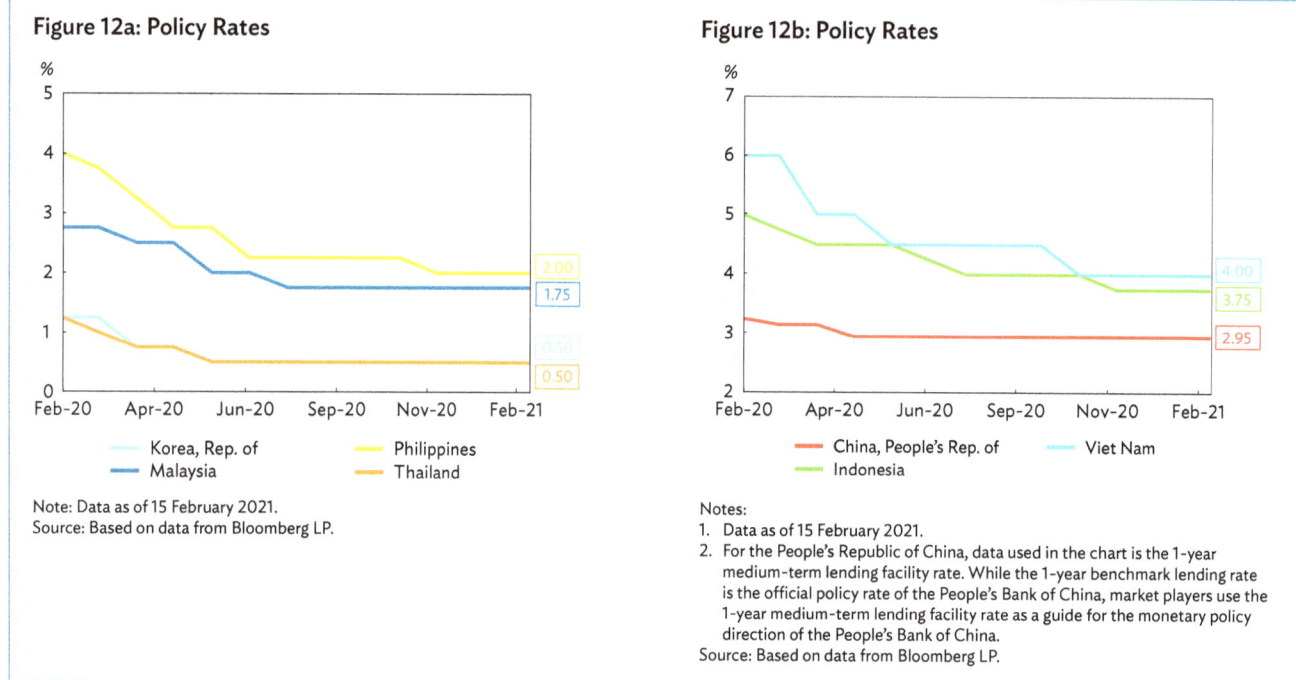

of Korea. Only the Philippines showed a sharp rise in inflation due to supply side issues (**Figure 11b**).

After having eased policy rates in the early part of 2020, all emerging East Asian central banks opted to leave monetary policy rates unchanged during the review period in order to assess the impact of previous monetary easing and given the improved economic outlook (**Figures 12a** and **12b**). However, Bank Indonesia on 18 February, reduced its policy rate by 25 basis points to support economic growth, and it downgraded its forecast for 2021 domestic growth to a range of 4.3%–5.3% from 4.8%–5.8%. Central banks in the region, however, may tighten monetary policy moving forward should inflation rise this year. In addition, the US recently passed a USD1.9 trillion stimulus bill, which could lead to a rise in US interest rates and subsequent tightening by the Federal Reserve. Other central banks might also follow to maintain parity and to avoid capital outflows.

Corporate spread fell on improved economic outlook.

The AAA-rated corporate versus government yield spread fell in all markets for which data are available between 31 December and 15 February on the back of improving investor optimism as confidence in the global economy grew (**Figure 13a**).

For lower-rated corporate bonds, the spreads were largely unchanged in the Republic of Korea and Thailand, but declined in the PRC and Malaysia (**Figure 13b**).

Figure 13a: Credit Spreads—Local Currency Corporates Rated AAA vs. Government Bonds

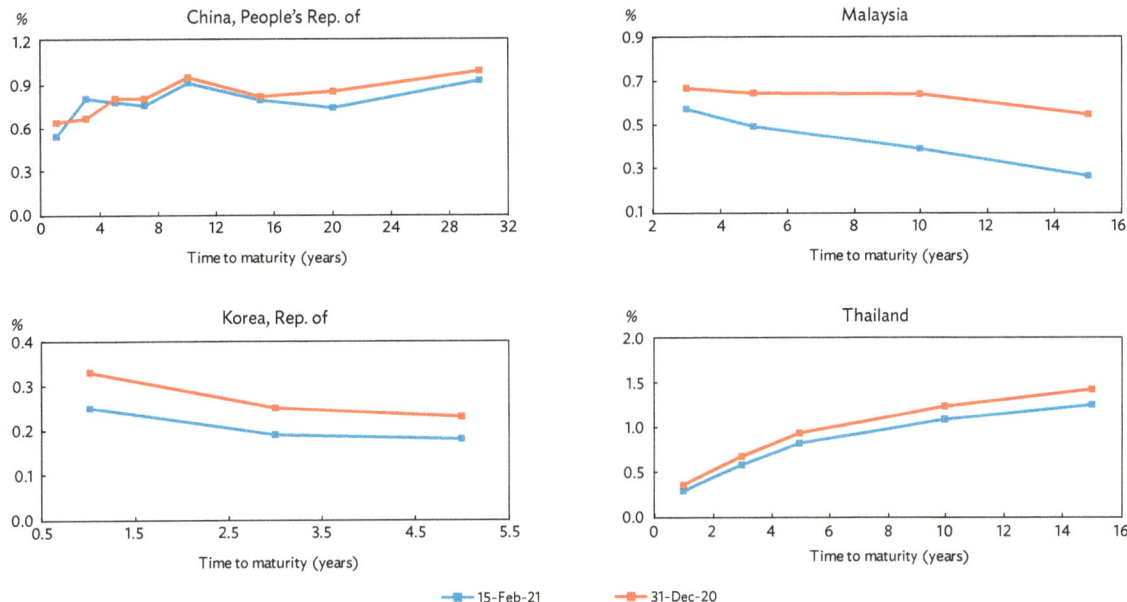

Notes:
1. Credit spreads are obtained by subtracting government yields from corporate indicative yields.
2. For the Republic of Korea, data on corporate bond yields are as of 24 December 2020 and 10 February 2021.
3. For Malaysia, data on corporate bonds yields are as of 31 December 2020 and 11 February 2021.
Sources: People's Republic of China (Bloomberg LP); Republic of Korea (KG Zeroin Corporation); Malaysia (Fully Automated System for Issuing/Tendering Bank Negara Malaysia); and Thailand (Bloomberg, LP).

Figure 13b: Credit Spreads—Lower-Rated Local Currency Corporates vs. AAA

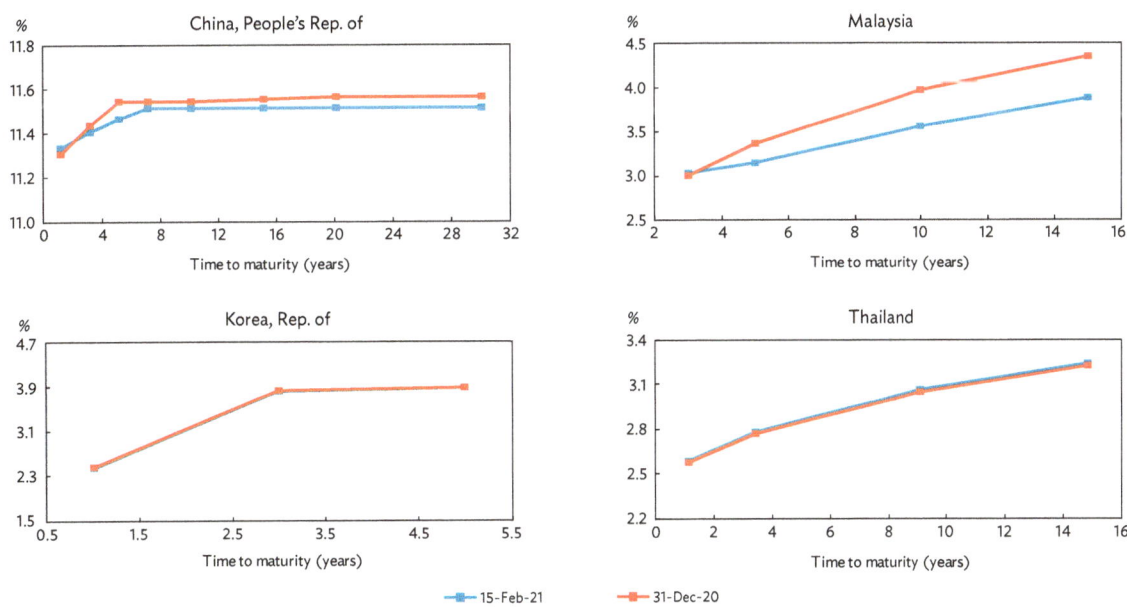

Notes:
1. Credit spreads are obtained by subtracting government yields from corporate indicative yields.
2. For the Republic of Korea, data on corporate bond yields are as of 24 December 2020 and 10 February 2021.
3. For Malaysia, data on corporate bonds yields are as of 31 December 2020 and 11 February 2021.
Sources: People's Republic of China (Bloomberg LP); Republic of Korea (KG Zeroin Corporation); Malaysia (Fully Automated System for Issuing/Tendering Bank Negara Malaysia); and Thailand (Bloomberg, LP).

Policy and Regulatory Developments

People's Republic of China

China Securities Regulatory Commission Release New Corporate Bond Guidelines

In February, the China Securities Regulatory Commission introduced new rules governing listed corporate bonds. Under the new rules, corporate bonds will no longer require a credit rating to be listed. In addition, a new registration system will be implemented.

Hong Kong, China

Hong Kong Monetary Authority Holds Countercyclical Capital Buffer at 1.0%

On 28 January, the Hong Kong Monetary Authority (HKMA) held the countercyclical capital buffer (CCyB) unchanged at 1.0%. The HKMA noted that the latest data based on indicators from the third quarter of 2020 signaled the need for a higher CCyB of 2.5%. However, the HKMA determined that, considering the high level of uncertainty facing the economy, it was more appropriate to hold the CCyB steady at 1.0% and continue to monitor the economic situation. A lower CCyB releases additional liquidity into the banking system by raising banks' lending capacity to support the economy. The CCyB is an integral part of the Basel III regulatory capital framework designed to increase the resilience of the banking sector in periods of excess credit growth.

Indonesia

Bank Indonesia Improves Calculation Methodology for the Jakarta Interbank Spot Dollar Rate

In February, Bank Indonesia announced a new regulation to improve the accuracy and relevancy of the Jakarta Interbank Spot Dollar Rate (JISDOR) and to align with international standards. The regulation, which will come into effect on 5 April 2021, calls for extending the data collection window for spot transactions used in the calculation of JISDOR and adjusting the publishing time of the JISDOR from morning to afternoon.

Republic of Korea

National Assembly Passes KRW558 Trillion 2021 Budget

On 2 December, the National Assembly of the Republic of Korea passed the KRW558.0 trillion 2021 budget. The total was KRW2.2 trillion higher than the proposed budget, which included a KRW7.5 trillion increase in allocation for policies related to easing the impact of the coronavirus disease (COVID-19) pandemic and other national priorities, while KRW5.3 trillion was removed from other programs. The 2021 budget is expected to result in a fiscal deficit of KRW75.4 trillion, or the equivalent of 3.7% of gross domestic product.

Republic of Korea Announces 2021 Economic Outlook and Policies

On 21 December, the Government of the Republic of Korea announced its economic outlook for 2021 along with its economic policies. The domestic economy is projected to grow 3.2% year-on-year on the back of improvements in domestic demand and export performance. Inflation is also expected to rise to 1.1% in 2021 from 0.5% in 2020. Economic policies in 2021 will focus on helping the economy regain growth momentum and supporting programs that will promote innovation and sustainable development. These include addressing continued uncertainties arising from the pandemic via expansionary fiscal policies to promote growth, vaccine distribution, and disease prevention.

Government Announces Measures to Strengthen Foreign Exchange Liquidity for Nonbank Financial Institutions

On 20 January, the Government of the Republic of Korea announced plans to further improve foreign exchange (FX) liquidity management and support mechanisms, particularly for nonbank financial institutions. This was the result of a short-term dollar shortage experienced in March 2020 amid the sudden impact of the pandemic on financial markets. Measures include a closer monitoring of nonbank financial institutions' risk management of

FX liquidity and derivatives transactions, introduction of three new indicators to assess FX liquidity, and improvements in existing regulations. Moreover, the government will strengthen the institutional framework, particularly the provision of a liquidity backstop, ensuring that FX liquidity is adequate in the event of another foreign liquidity crunch.

Malaysia

Financial Markets Committee to Develop Alternative Reference Rate for Malaysia

In December, Bank Negara Malaysia's Financial Market Committee was tasked to head the development of an alternative reference rate for the Malaysian financial market. The new reference rate will eventually replace, or be used together with, the current Kuala Lumpur Interbank Offered Rate as the committee deliberates its continued use. The move is in line with the Financial Stability Board's recommendation encouraging financial benchmark reforms around the world to improve the integrity of global reference rates.

Bank Negara Malaysia Extends Statutory Reserve Requirement Rule

On 20 January, Bank Negara Malaysia extended until the end of 2022 the policy of allowing banks to utilize Malaysian Government Securities and Government Investment Issues to meet the 2.0% statutory reserve requirement threshold. The extension aims to promote bank liquidity to support their activities during the pandemic.

Philippines

Bangko Sentral ng Pilipinas Approves Another PHP540 Billion Loan to the Government

On 28 December, the Bangko Sentral ng Pilipinas approved another PHP540 billion loan to the central government to augment its pandemic funds. The loan will be settled within 3 months, which can be extended for another 3 months, and bears no interest. This is the third advance to the government from the central bank following the loans granted in March and October 2020. The Bayanihan to Recover as One Act increases the amount the central bank can lend to the central government from 20% to 30% of its average annual revenue, or PHP850 billion.

Financial Institutions Strategic Transfer Act Signed into Law

On 17 February, the Financial Institutions Strategic Transfer Act was signed into law. The act will allow financial institutions like banks to offload nonperforming assets to asset management companies, thereby improving financial institutions' liquidity to allow them to provide more credit to businesses. The law will ease the nonperforming loan ratios of banks, which have increased as a result of the impact of the COVID-19 pandemic.

Singapore

Singapore to Transition from Swap Offer Rate and Singapore Interbank Offer Rate to Singapore Overnight Rate Average

In December, Monetary Authority of Singapore (MAS) empowered the committee in charge of overseeing the economy's transition from the Swap Offer Rate and Singapore Interbank Offer Rate to the Singapore Overnight Rate Average. The move came as the Association of Banks in Singapore, the Singapore Foreign Exchange Market Committee, and the steering committee recommended last year to discontinue the use of the Singapore Interbank Offer Rate in favor of the Singapore Overnight Rate Average.

Monetary Authority of Singapore and Federal Reserve Extend Bilateral Swap Agreement

In December, MAS and the United States (US) Federal Reserve extended to 30 September 2021 their USD60 billion bilateral swap agreement. In line with this, MAS also extended to 30 September the duration of its US dollar facility, which offers up to USD60 billion in funding to banks. The swap agreement aims to enhance US dollar lending to businesses in Singapore to support their operations during the pandemic. The effort also ensures financial liquidity and stability.

Thailand

Bank Indonesia and the Bank of Thailand Expand Local Currency Settlement Framework

On 21 December, Bank Indonesia and the Bank of Thailand announced the expansion of the rupiah–baht settlement framework as part of continuing efforts to promote wider use of local currencies to facilitate trade and investment between Indonesia and Thailand. Direct investment is now included as an underlying transaction covered by the local currency settlement framework. Relevant foreign exchange rules and regulations were also relaxed through more flexible documentation requirements. The two central banks appointed additional commercial banks in their respective countries to support the implementation of the expanded rupiah–baht settlement framework.

Viet Nam

Government of Viet Nam Issues New Corporate Bond Market Regulation

On 31 October, the Government of Viet Nam issued Decree No. 153/2020/ND-CP, which regulates the private offering and trading of corporate bonds in the domestic market and the offering of corporate bonds in the international market effective 1 January 2021. This replaced Decree No. 81/2020/ND-CP that came into effect on 1 September 2020. The previous decree tightened the standards of corporate bond issuance but resulted in the bond market losing growth momentum after its implementation.

Environmental, Social, and Governance Bonds in ASEAN+3

The amount of environmental, social, and governance (ESG) bonds outstanding in ASEAN+3 has steadily risen in recent quarters (**Figure 14**).[8] At the end of December, the outstanding stock of ESG bonds in the region reached USD265.8 billion on growth of 6.3% quarter-on-quarter and 34.8% year-on-year.

Green bonds dominate the regional ESG bond stock, accounting for about 76.4% of ESG bonds outstanding and totaling USD203.1 billion at the end of December. However, green bonds' share of the total ESG bond stock declined in 2020 due to the rapid rise in issuance of social bonds and sustainability bonds. Social bonds' share of the total ESG bond stock rose from only 4.9% at the end of 2019 to 11.6% at the end of 2020, while the share of sustainability bonds increased from 8.1% to 11.9% in the same period.

Corporate bonds dominate the regional ESG bond market, accounting for nearly 90% of aggregate ESG bonds outstanding at the end of December.[9] Green bonds and sustainability bonds, in particular, are largely corporate bonds (**Figure 15**). In contrast, social bonds have largely been issued by corporates with government affiliations.

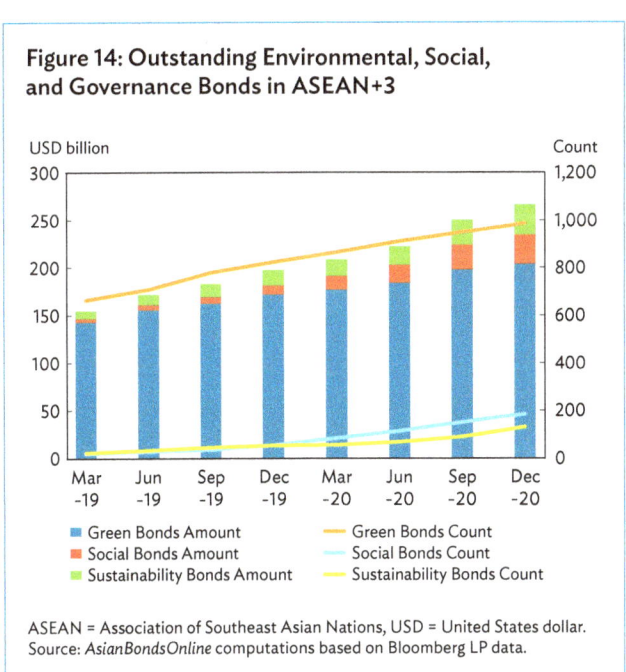

Figure 14: Outstanding Environmental, Social, and Governance Bonds in ASEAN+3

ASEAN = Association of Southeast Asian Nations, USD = United States dollar.
Source: *AsianBondsOnline* computations based on Bloomberg LP data.

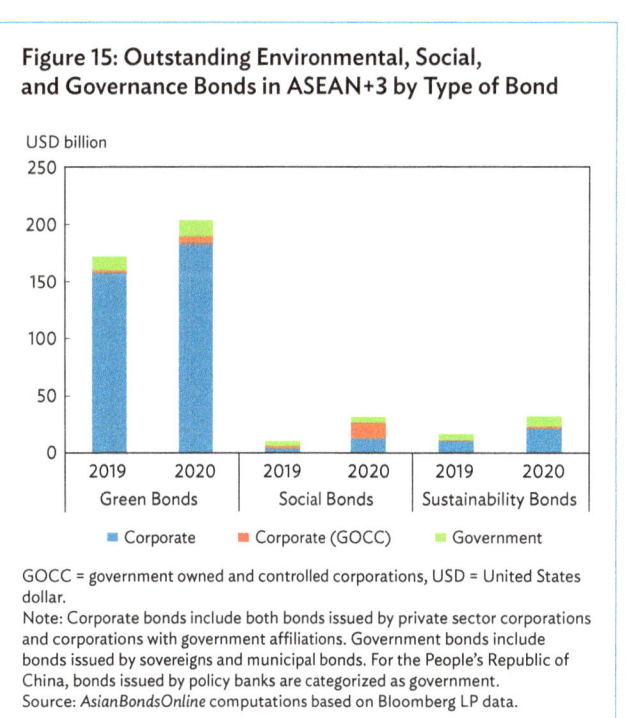

Figure 15: Outstanding Environmental, Social, and Governance Bonds in ASEAN+3 by Type of Bond

GOCC = government owned and controlled corporations, USD = United States dollar.
Note: Corporate bonds include both bonds issued by private sector corporations and corporations with government affiliations. Government bonds include bonds issued by sovereigns and municipal bonds. For the People's Republic of China, bonds issued by policy banks are categorized as government.
Source: *AsianBondsOnline* computations based on Bloomberg LP data.

---

[8] ESG bond data were obtained from Bloomberg using the SRCH function. ESG bonds are labeled as such per Bloomberg's "use of proceeds" to identify green, social, and sustainability bonds. In addition, bonds with a Bloomberg New Energy Finance Rating of A1 are included as green bonds.
[9] Corporate bonds include both bonds issued by private sector corporations and corporations with government affiliations.

By type of issuer, the majority of green bonds and sustainability bonds have been issued by firms from the financial sector, which accounted for issuance shares of 50% and 71%, respectively, at the end of December 2020 (**Figures 16**). Governments remain the dominant issuers of social bonds.

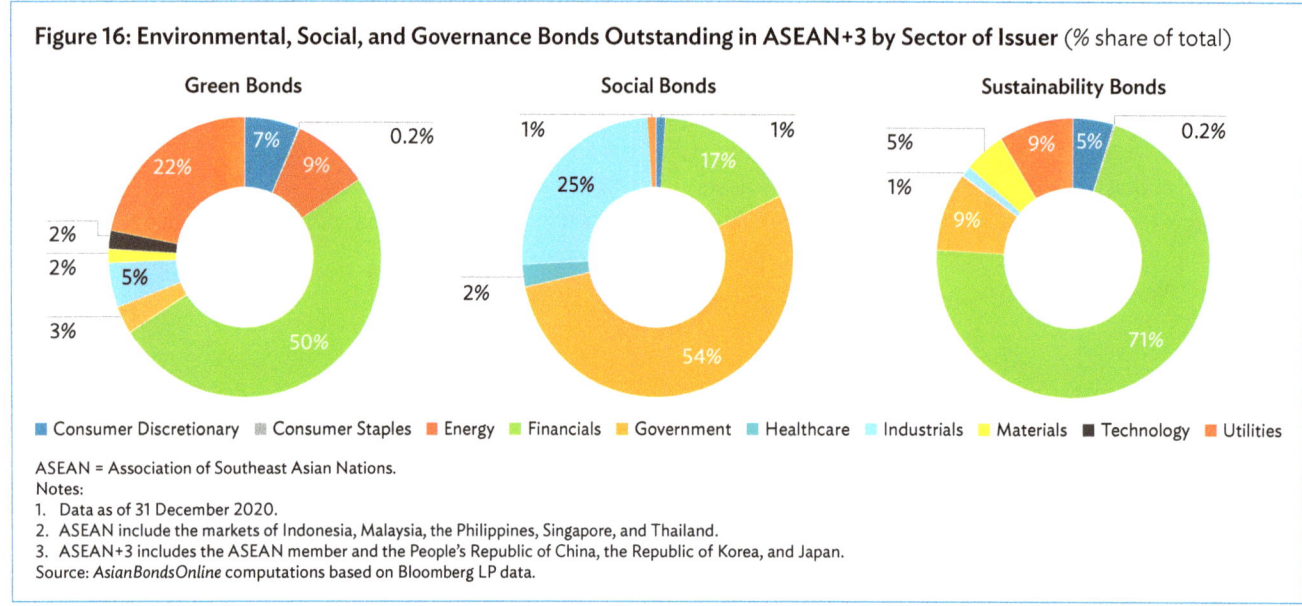

Figure 16: Environmental, Social, and Governance Bonds Outstanding in ASEAN+3 by Sector of Issuer (% share of total)

ASEAN = Association of Southeast Asian Nations.
Notes:
1. Data as of 31 December 2020.
2. ASEAN include the markets of Indonesia, Malaysia, the Philippines, Singapore, and Thailand.
3. ASEAN+3 includes the ASEAN member and the People's Republic of China, the Republic of Korea, and Japan.
Source: *AsianBondsOnline* computations based on Bloomberg LP data.

In terms of regional market share by economy, the People's Republic of China was the largest issuer of green bonds at the end of December 2020 with a share of 72% of the region's total outstanding green bonds (**Figure 17**). Japan was the next largest with a share of 11%. ASEAN markets had an aggregate 6% share of green bonds outstanding.

For social bonds, the Republic of Korea was the majority issuer at the end of December 2020 with a regional market share of 52%, followed by Japan with a share of 45%. ASEAN markets had an aggregate share of 0.06%.

The Republic of Korea was also the dominant issuer of sustainability bonds at the end of December 2020, with a share of 40%. Japan was next largest with a share of 33%. ASEAN markets were relatively larger issuers of sustainability bonds than other ESG bond types with a regional share of 19%.

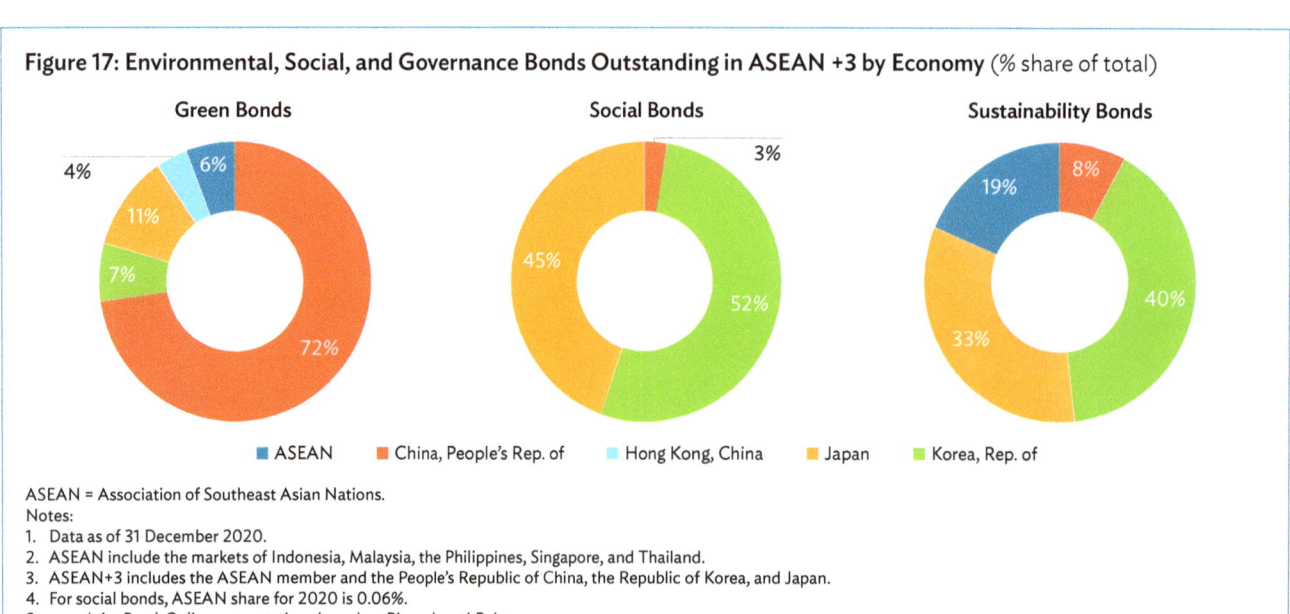

Figure 17: Environmental, Social, and Governance Bonds Outstanding in ASEAN +3 by Economy (% share of total)

ASEAN = Association of Southeast Asian Nations.
Notes:
1. Data as of 31 December 2020.
2. ASEAN include the markets of Indonesia, Malaysia, the Philippines, Singapore, and Thailand.
3. ASEAN+3 includes the ASEAN member and the People's Republic of China, the Republic of Korea, and Japan.
4. For social bonds, ASEAN share for 2020 is 0.06%.
Source: *AsianBondsOnline* computations based on Bloomberg LP data.

ESG bonds in ASEAN+3 markets were mostly issued in local currency (LCY). In the green bond market, LCY bonds accounted for about 67% of the total outstanding at the end of December 2020 (**Figure 18**). While in the social bond market, LCY bonds represented 73% of the total. In contrast, a majority (60%) of sustainability bonds were issued in foreign currency.

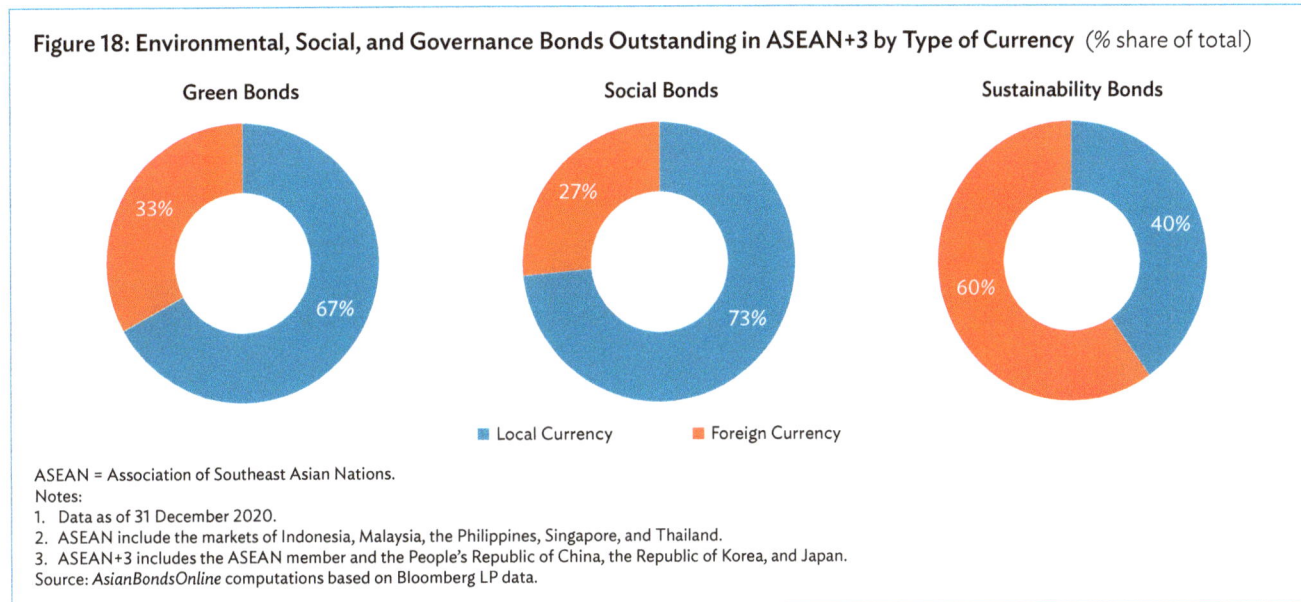

Figure 18: Environmental, Social, and Governance Bonds Outstanding in ASEAN+3 by Type of Currency (% share of total)

ASEAN = Association of Southeast Asian Nations.
Notes:
1. Data as of 31 December 2020.
2. ASEAN include the markets of Indonesia, Malaysia, the Philippines, Singapore, and Thailand.
3. ASEAN+3 includes the ASEAN member and the People's Republic of China, the Republic of Korea, and Japan.
Source: *AsianBondsOnline* computations based on Bloomberg LP data.

Social Bonds—Recent Developments and Trends

A Primer and Recent Developments in Asia

Harnessing the power of private capital to address compelling societal needs is critical to meeting the challenges of developing Asia.[10] Social bonds, which raise funds to create social as well as financial value, are instruments with a vital role to play in spurring recovery from the coronavirus disease (COVID-19) crisis and future socioeconomic progress.

Under the framework developed by the International Capital Market Association (ICMA), there are three types of environmental, social, and governance (ESG) bond instruments: (i) green bonds, which raise capital for projects with environmental and climate benefits; (ii) social bonds, which raise funds for projects with social benefits; and (iii) sustainability bonds, which raise funds for projects with both green and social benefits. In June 2020, the ICMA expanded its list of eligible projects and target communities relevant to social bonds in response to the rapid growth of the social bond market amid the COVID-19 pandemic.

Driven by growing investor demand for instruments that deliver ESG value, equity and bond markets have innovated over the past 2 decades to develop a number of sustainable finance instruments. The global bond markets have embraced this movement; ESG-linked bond issuance jumped 33% year-on-year (y-o-y) to USD330 billion in 2019 and another 58% y-o-y to USD522 billion in 2020, while outstanding ESG bonds passed the USD1 trillion threshold in the middle of 2020. The ESG market initially was dominated by green bonds, but social bonds experienced exceptional growth in 2020, partly due to the to the strong demand for social bonds to finance activities that mitigate the fallout from the pandemic.

This development is ushering in a new era of explosive growth for ESG-labeled bonds in general and social bonds in particular.

Economic and social development needs in developing Asia highlight the urgency—as well as the opportunity—for creating a robust social bond market in the region. With the stunning impact of COVID-19 still unfolding, the Asian Development Bank assesses that the pandemic has already taken a heavy toll on the region's developing economies. In December 2020, the Asian Development Bank forecast that developing Asia's gross domestic product would contract by 0.4% in 2020, the region's weakest economic performance since 1961.[11] This is expected to be followed by a 6.8% expansion in 2021, with downside risks—rather than upside potential—prevailing.

The fallout from the pandemic has been disproportionately damaging to vulnerable and underserved people and communities throughout the region, as vital areas such as tourism, the informal economy, and small and medium-sized enterprises (SMEs) in particular have been affected. This has exacerbated the funding gap needed to attain the United Nations (UN) Sustainable Development Goals. Prior to the pandemic, the UN warned that developing economies in Asia and the Pacific faced an annual funding gap of USD1.5 trillion compared with what was needed to achieve the Sustainable Development Goals. Recent developments underscore the opportunity for social bonds to help close this funding gap by financing social investments and improving the quality of project outcomes through a commitment to measuring and reporting impact.

Global social bond issuance saw tremendous growth in 2020, as the COVID-19 pandemic and economic

---

[10] This section was written by Jason Mortimer (Head of Sustainable Investment—Fixed Income) at Nomura Asset Management and Jane Hughes (Professor) at Simmons University (United States). The content is based on Asian Development Bank. 2021. *Primer on Social Bonds and Recent Developments in Asia.* https://www.adb.org/publications/social-bonds-recent-developments-asia. Developing Asia comprises the 46 developing member economies of the Asian Development Bank. The information and views expressed in this report are made in the authors' personal capacity and is not in any way a product of or reflect the views of Nomura Asset Management or any entity in the Nomura Group of companies. This material does not in any way constitute an offer to sell or buy any financial product, nor is it a disclosure document based on the Japan Financial Instruments and Exchange Act.
[11] Developing Asia comprises the 46 developing member economies of the Asian Development Bank.

shutdowns greatly increased market supply and demand for financing response and recovery efforts. Following y-o-y growth of 28% in 2018 and 44% in 2019, the issuance of global social bonds surged to nearly USD150 billion equivalent in 2020 (**Figure 19**). In comparison, global issuance of green bonds, which have typically dominated the labeled ESG bond market, rose 4% y-o-y to USD239 billion equivalent in 2020.

Social bond issuance in Asia has consistently lagged behind European issuance, but recent growth in the region has been impressive. From 2017 to 2019, annual Asian social bond issuance grew from 12% to 38% of the global total (excluding supranational issuance) before falling back to 23% in 2020 due to exceptionally high issuance from Europe, particularly France. However, Asia is now consistently the second most active region in terms of social bond issuance, as annual issuance grew 22.3 times from 2017 to 2020, compared with growth of 9.8 times for Europe and 14.3 times for global issuance excluding Asia. Nonetheless, the Asian social bond market is still less than half the size of the European market, and the need—and opportunity—for even faster growth is apparent. In the Asia social bond market, issuance so far has been dominated by government-related agency issuers in high-income economies such as Japan and the Republic of Korea, where such issuance makes up 41% and 48% of the entire outstanding Asian social bond market, respectively (**Figure 20**).

While philanthropic and supranational institutions are significant issuers of social bonds, they also help to develop the market ecosystem and support prospective participants to enter the market. Governments, including both policymakers and regulators, also are key to ecosystem development. Together, these groups can provide market education, technical assistance, thought

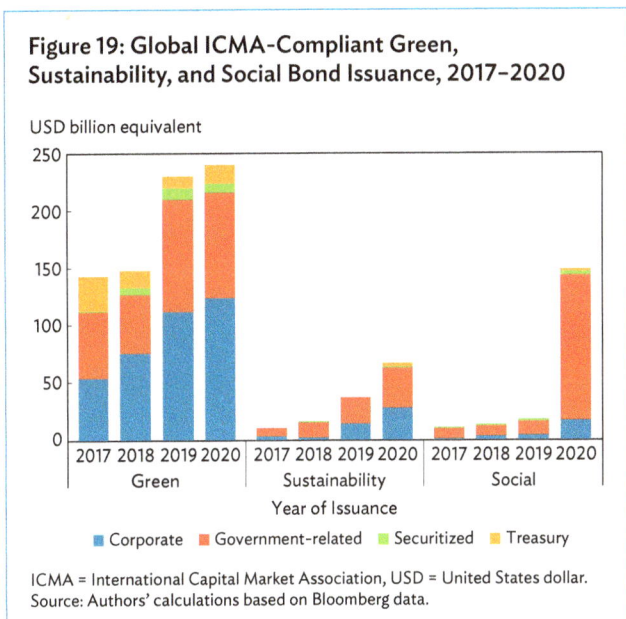

Figure 19: Global ICMA-Compliant Green, Sustainability, and Social Bond Issuance, 2017–2020

ICMA = International Capital Market Association, USD = United States dollar.
Source: Authors' calculations based on Bloomberg data.

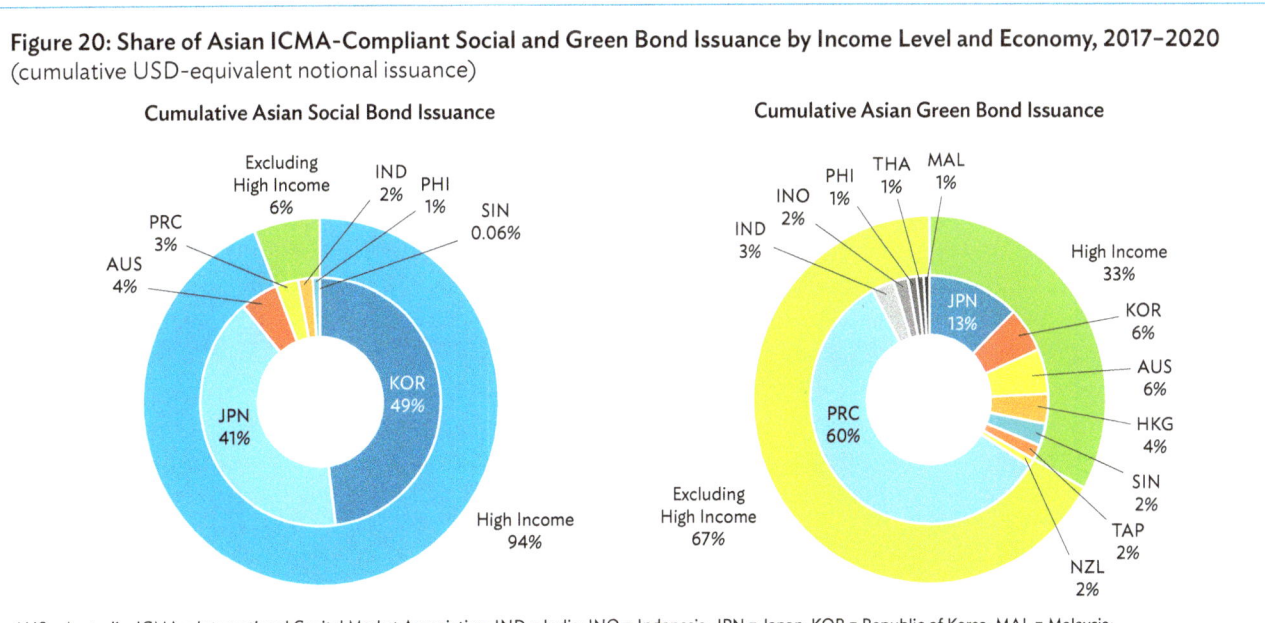

Figure 20: Share of Asian ICMA-Compliant Social and Green Bond Issuance by Income Level and Economy, 2017–2020
(cumulative USD-equivalent notional issuance)

AUS = Australia; ICMA = International Capital Market Association; IND = India; INO = Indonesia; JPN = Japan; KOR = Republic of Korea; MAL = Malaysia; NZL = New Zealand; PHI = Philippines; PRC = People's Republic of China; SIN = Singapore; TAP = Taipei,China; THA = Thailand; USD = United States dollar.
Source: Authors' calculations based on Bloomberg data.

leadership, and an enabling regulatory framework; they can also take an active role in crowding in private capital by offering first-loss capital or capital guarantees.

It seems likely that neither investors' nor issuers' attraction to social bonds will fade with COVID-19. Obstacles to market growth, however, include the lack of a standardized set of metrics to measure impact, which leads to concerns about "social washing" (i.e., overstating the social value of a bond); a need for higher issuance volume and diversity (i.e., more corporate issuers); a lack of training among financial advisers; and the lack of a social bond framework—which can take time, money, and manpower to develop—for many of Asia's sovereigns and corporates that would like to tap the market.

There is undoubtedly an urgent and compelling case for the development of a robust social bond market in Asia. Harnessing the power of private capital to meet critical social needs is an opportunity for both issuers and investors to address these needs in a financial context. While the COVID-19 pandemic will eventually recede, one lasting impact may well be its catalytic effect on the development of social bonds worldwide. 2020 was the year when mainstream investors "discovered" social investments; this presents an opportunity for investors to expand their commitment to this area and advance the possibilities of what social investing can deliver in terms of real-world outcomes over a broad range of issues.

A Nascent Opportunity for ESG Investing

The COVID-19 pandemic has amplified inequality.[12] The crisis may push 71 million more people into extreme poverty. Highlighting the importance of social issues, the pandemic has created sizable new investment opportunities as social theme becomes increasingly important for investors. In North America, the social pillar outperformed the environmental and governance pillars in the first quarter of 2020. Furthermore, Asian and European institutional investors are paying more attention to the social pillar in their investment strategy (**Figure 21**).

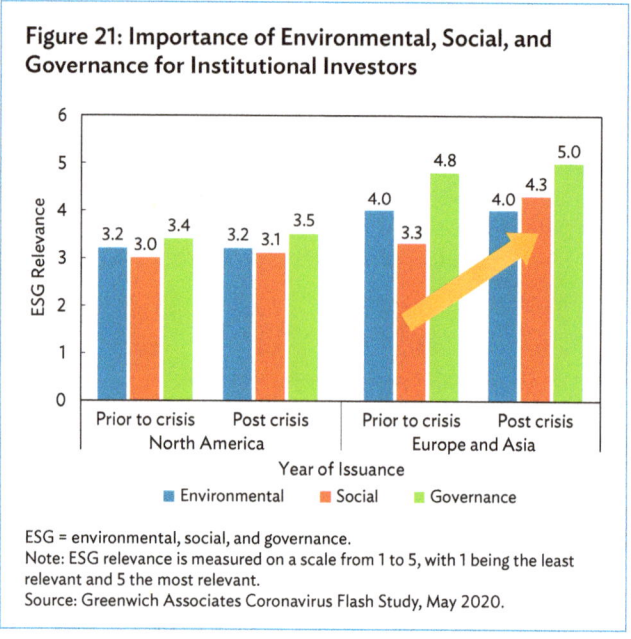

Figure 21: Importance of Environmental, Social, and Governance for Institutional Investors

ESG = environmental, social, and governance.
Note: ESG relevance is measured on a scale from 1 to 5, with 1 being the least relevant and 5 the most relevant.
Source: Greenwich Associates Coronavirus Flash Study, May 2020.

Social bond markets grow rapidly since COVID-19 outbreak. Social bonds account for approximately 15% of the USD1,366 billion in cumulative sustainable fixed-income issuance. Europe is the dominant social bond issuer, accounting for 45% of new social bond issuance in 2020. However, issuance in Asia and the Pacific and North America is on the rise with the Asian market experiencing the most rapid growth.

There are a number of reasons why institutional investors are showing greater interest in social bonds. First, investing in social bonds does not sacrifice returns. The risk-return profile of social bonds is comparable to vanilla bonds from the same issuer.

Importantly, social bonds provide a platform for engaged dialogue with corporate issuers. Such active ownership enables investors to encourage issuers to prioritize long-term sustainability in their business operations.

Furthermore, institutional investors can request issuers to report about the social outcomes of the investment projects. This gives investors clearer information about the measurable social impact of their investments while reducing the risk of social impact washing.

---

[12] This section is based on *Social Bonds: A Nascent Opportunity for ESG Investing* written by Elodie Laugel (Chief Responsible Investment Officer) and Isabelle Vic-Philippe (Head of Euro Aggregate) of Amundi.

To sum up, the pronounced impact of COVID-19 on the poor has exacerbated inequality. However, one positive consequence has been the accelerated growth of social bonds, which can generate positive social outcomes. Going forward, the growth of social bond markets is likely to be sustainable because they offer substantial benefits for investors. The prospects for further expansion are especially promising in Asia, where the markets remain relatively small despite rapid recent growth.

Promoting Social Bonds for Impact Investments in Asia

With the volume of global social bond issuance having achieved a new record in 2020, it becomes critically important to understand how to optimize use of these financial instruments, specifically in terms of which social issues to address and which project types to target to maximize deep and lasting impact.[13] It is crucial that Asia gets this right so that social bonds are used to "build back better" and not for minimally impactful projects or, worse, for social washing.

As the prefix "pan" indicates, the COVID-19 pandemic is much more than a health crisis; indeed, it affects virtually all aspects of human development. It has magnified the pernicious effects of poverty and inequality, and led to much greater suffering among vulnerable communities as compared to the better-off. Recovery work can thus be viewed as double-pronged: (i) meeting urgent short-term needs such as employment generation, support for small business, and healthcare provision; and (ii) launching longer-term public works programs to reduce poverty and develop resilience to future shocks.

Along with a more than sevenfold y-o-y increase in social bond issuance in 2020, there has also been a significant change in the pattern of target areas for social bond use of proceeds. Most notably, there was a shift from the pre-2020 focus on affordable housing to more pandemic-related project categories such as education and training (especially retraining for unemployed workers), and crisis alleviation efforts (a new category in the 2020 Social Bond Principles that is primarily related to employment generation). In Asia, social bond issuance has always

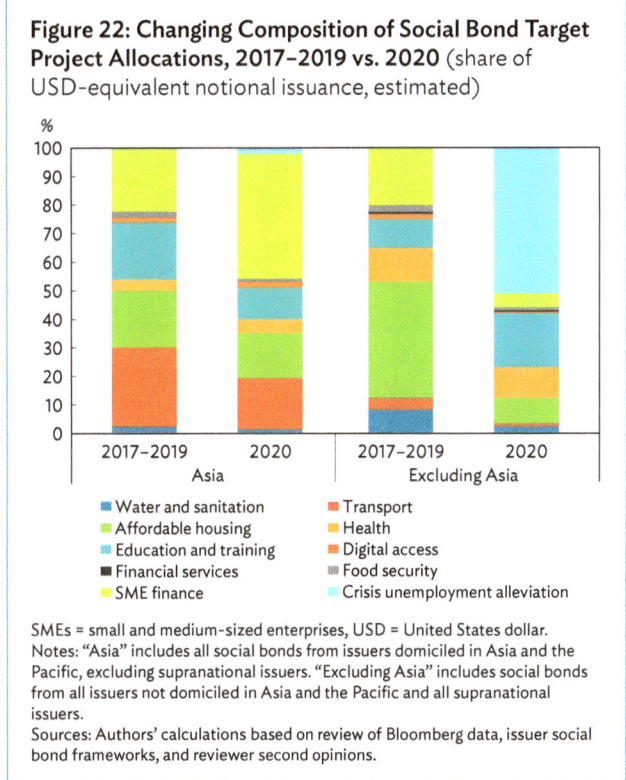

Figure 22: Changing Composition of Social Bond Target Project Allocations, 2017–2019 vs. 2020 (share of USD-equivalent notional issuance, estimated)

SMEs = small and medium-sized enterprises, USD = United States dollar.
Notes: "Asia" includes all social bonds from issuers domiciled in Asia and the Pacific, excluding supranational issuers. "Excluding Asia" includes social bonds from all issuers not domiciled in Asia and the Pacific and all supranational issuers.
Sources: Authors' calculations based on review of Bloomberg data, issuer social bond frameworks, and reviewer second opinions.

focused on socioeconomic areas such as SME finance and transport access, representing 37% and 21%, respectively, of allocated social bond issuance from 2017 to 2020 (**Figure 22**).

Moving on from the immediate need to save lives in the midst of a pandemic, medium- to longer-term healthcare needs top the list of priority issue areas for social bond financing. The pandemic has exposed the vast weaknesses, inequities, and shortages associated with healthcare in many developing economies; surely, a build-back-better approach must be founded on a resilient and equitable healthcare system to prevent and mitigate future crises.

COVID-19 has also exposed critical vulnerabilities in global food and water systems by straining supplies, disrupting food chains, and increasing food insecurity for millions of people. Frequent handwashing is among the most effective measures in containing COVID-19 and other diseases, but chronic underinvestment in water infrastructure has left

---

[13] This section is based on Asian Development Bank. Forthcoming. *Promoting Social Bonds for Impact Investments in Asia*, which was written by Jason Mortimer (Head of Sustainable Investment—Fixed Income) at Nomura Asset Management and Jane Hughes (Professor) at Simmons University (United States). The information and views expressed in this report are made in the author's personal capacity only and is not in any way a product of, or reflect the views of, Nomura Asset Management or any entity in the Nomura Group of companies. This material does not in any way constitute an offer to sell or buy any financial product and is not a disclosure document based on the Japan Financial Instruments and Exchange Act.

hundreds of millions without access to running water and soap at home. This is a wake-up call alerting the world to the potential for improved water and nutritional systems in the developing world to fundamentally improve global health outcomes for everyone.

Providing support to SMEs is a short-term necessity to get both businesses and people back on their feet again after the demand shock of the pandemic and lockdown policies. SMEs account for more than 96% of all businesses in Asia and the Pacific, and more than two-thirds of the private sector workforce. Even before the pandemic, SMEs faced a number of critical obstacles, most importantly their lack of access to finance. We estimate that 100% of Asian social bond issuance (excluding issuers in high-income economies) in 2020 was allocated to SME financing, which is not surprising given the nature of the shock and economic structure of the region (**Figure 23**).

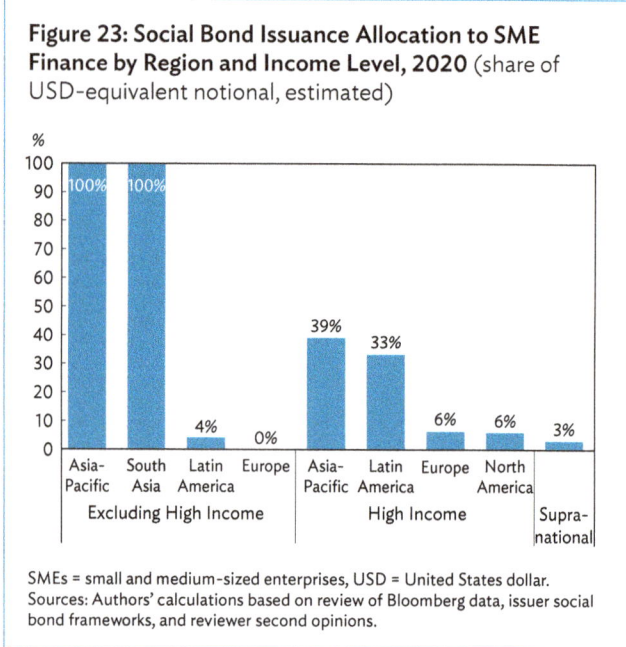

Figure 23: Social Bond Issuance Allocation to SME Finance by Region and Income Level, 2020 (share of USD-equivalent notional, estimated)

SMEs = small and medium-sized enterprises, USD = United States dollar.
Sources: Authors' calculations based on review of Bloomberg data, issuer social bond frameworks, and reviewer second opinions.

While it is imperative to raise funds to meet the short- to medium-term needs of people and businesses in the wake of the pandemic, it is just as imperative to address the need for greater levels of resilience in advance of the next crisis—and, even better, to prevent the next crisis. Much of developing Asia is considered to be lacking in the area of resilience. The UN Economic and Social Commission for Asia and the Pacific estimates that over 60% of the population of Asia and the Pacific lacks access to social protection, as do 70% of workers in the region's informal sector. Poverty increases vulnerability to shocks in a number of ways, as the pandemic has amply demonstrated.

Perhaps the greatest opportunity for impactful investment is education, especially girls' education. This is not only a basic human right, but it is also one of the most effective ways to drive sustainable development, improve health, reduce conflict, and save lives. Even before the pandemic, girls' access to education was limited in a number of Asian economies. The pandemic has made a difficult situation much worse, as girls who were forced out of school by the pandemic are much less likely than boys to return to their studies. If this trend is not reversed, it could have repercussions for many years to come. This, in turn, highlights the pressing need for innovative finance to advance gender equity, as the pandemic has had a dramatically gender-differentiated impact throughout Asia and the Pacific.

Poverty and inequality underpin many of the abovementioned social ills and present unique intersectional dimensions. While poverty has declined substantially in Asia and the Pacific over the past several decades, its rate of reduction has slowed since 2010, and the pandemic is certain to reverse a number of those gains. Social ills are deeply and fundamentally intersectional; many problems bleed into and are connected to others, so solving these problems demands an intersectional approach.

The knotty and unresolved question of social impact measurement is central to the theme of building back better. Social bonds are only as good as the impact they help to achieve, so it is imperative that they and all other ESG-linked instruments are assessed by as rigorous a method of social impact measurement as is practicable. But practicability in this area is a serious constraint and thus it is not surprising that social impact measurement is by no means a settled issue. There is much experimentation and innovation going on in the field, much of it useful and instructional, but there is as yet no widespread coalescence around a single model of social impact assessment.

To promote more standardized impact measurement, an ICMA working group has released a draft version of recommendations for social bond issuers. In particular, it proposes standardized reporting based on ICMA project categories and subcategories, project allocation share, target population, project lifetime, and measurements based on the output, outcomes, and/or impact of projects; but it does not propose a definitive list of such impact measurements.

Some discomfort around this is appropriate, as social impact measurement is to some extent an exercise in quantifying the unquantifiable. None of this, however, lessens the importance and value of impact measurement.

It will be challenging for policymakers, issuers, and investors to determine which issue areas should be addressed through social bond financing. Without standardized impact measurement methodologies, market participants' ability to compare projects is limited; and with so many high-priority needs, hard decisions will be necessary. The good news is that social bonds have proven themselves to be valuable instruments for directing private capital to these myriad priorities, while impact measurement is improving and deepening throughout the industry. From resilience to SME support, from gender equity to healthcare, social bonds will be an essential tool for financing the work needed for developing Asia to build back better.

AsianBondsOnline 2020 Bond Market Liquidity Survey

Introduction

Liquidity is an integral aspect of bond markets. Good market liquidity is a key advantage for investors, as it keeps funds from being locked up and allows investors to quickly liquidate bonds when needed. For issuers, good liquidity allows them to issue bonds with longer maturities to mitigate prepayment risk. Hence, a key aspect in the development of a well-functioning bond market is to ensure both breadth and depth in bond market transactions, as well as doing so at a low transaction cost. If there is a lack of liquidity in bond markets, issuance from corporates and governments, and readiness to invest from investors, will be curtailed.

As part of AsianBondsOnline's efforts to provide information on local currency (LCY) bond markets, a bond market liquidity survey is conducted on an annual basis. The goal of the survey is to provide a snapshot of the state of liquidity in emerging East Asian bond markets.[14] The survey helps identify areas of weakness in each of the region's bond markets that could aid key bond market stakeholders, particularly policy makers and financial market regulators, to undertake reforms and/or address areas for development. For the 2020 survey, a shortened version compared to past surveys was conducted. The survey was undertaken solely via email as the coronavirus disease (COVID-19) outbreak restricted us from conducting market visits and face-to-face interviews.

As in past years, the survey was targeted for various bond market participants such as bond traders from financial institutions, financial market brokers, research houses, fund managers, and bond pricing agencies. The survey period commenced from late November through the middle of December 2020, with the aim of capturing the impact of the COVID-19 outbreak on the region's bond markets.

The survey comprises two parts: a quantitative section and a qualitive section, each covering LCY government and corporate bonds. The quantitative section analyzes market data on bid–ask spreads and transaction sizes, which are used as measures for assessing the liquidity conditions in each of the region's LCY bond markets. The qualitative section presents the overall perception of market participants on the degree of development of their respective bond market based on identified structural issues.

Both advanced and emerging economies were roiled by the COVID-19 pandemic. Government efforts to mitigate the spread of the disease, such as lockdowns and quarantines, as well as reduced consumer demand, led to a contraction in economic output in 2020. Financial markets were also affected, with some markets experiencing a decline in liquidity and heightened bankruptcy risks. This led to central governments and central banks in the region engaging in measures to help support the economy and boost liquidity in financial markets. Central banks also implemented accommodative monetary policy measures.

In some markets, liquidity and overall trading activity declined as a result of the negative sentiment and impact of COVID-19. An increase in government bonds as a result of fiscal stimulus measures also helped drain liquidity. But in other cases, positive investor sentiment for that particular economy and/or the accommodative measures of central banks helped boost liquidity.

The majority of survey participants noted that overall bond market liquidity in emerging East Asia increased during 2020. Some 53% of participants said that overall bond market liquidity improved versus 2019, while 38% said that liquidity had worsened (**Figure 24**). Only 9% said that liquidity remained the same.

However, on a per market basis, liquidity conditions were deemed mixed in 2020. Most survey participants from the People's Republic of China (PRC), Indonesia, Malaysia, and Viet Nam observed improved conditions over the previous year. On the other hand, participants from

---

[14] Emerging East Asia comprises the People's Republic of China; Hong Kong, China; Indonesia; the Republic of Korea; Malaysia; the Philippines; Singapore; Thailand; and Viet Nam.

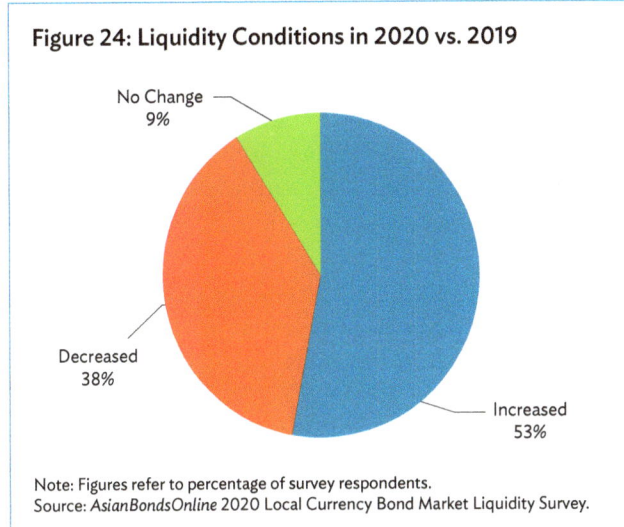

Figure 24: Liquidity Conditions in 2020 vs. 2019

No Change 9%
Decreased 38%
Increased 53%

Note: Figures refer to percentage of survey respondents.
Source: AsianBondsOnline 2020 Local Currency Bond Market Liquidity Survey.

the Republic of Korea, the Philippines, Singapore, and Thailand noted decreased liquidity. Survey respondents from Hong Kong, China perceived that there was no change in liquidity conditions in 2020 versus 2019.

Market participants were also asked about various factors that affected liquidity conditions in the bond market in 2020. The three biggest drivers of liquidity were market sentiment, the COVID-19 pandemic, and movements in bond yields (**Figure 25**). It was also observed that among various factors, developments relating to the euro area had the least impact on emerging East Asia's bond markets. Factors relating to Brexit and the euro area's economy and monetary policy were only mentioned by a handful of participants.

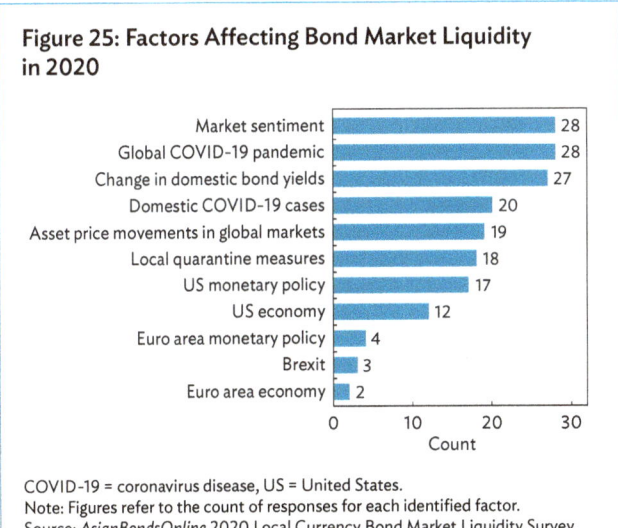

Figure 25: Factors Affecting Bond Market Liquidity in 2020

Factor	Count
Market sentiment	28
Global COVID-19 pandemic	28
Change in domestic bond yields	27
Domestic COVID-19 cases	20
Asset price movements in global markets	19
Local quarantine measures	18
US monetary policy	17
US economy	12
Euro area monetary policy	4
Brexit	3
Euro area economy	2

COVID-19 = coronavirus disease, US = United States.
Note: Figures refer to the count of responses for each identified factor.
Source: AsianBondsOnline 2020 Local Currency Bond Market Liquidity Survey.

Quantitative Indicators for Government Bond Markets

Figure 26 presents the quarterly turnover ratios for emerging East Asian markets where data are available. A similar pattern in nearly all markets were noted where the quarterly turnover ratio was the highest in the first quarter (Q1) of 2020 before exhibiting a decline. Turnover ratios in the region's government bond markets were mostly down in the second quarter (Q2) of 2020 as markets experienced the full impact of quarantine measures, affecting both investor sentiment and drying up liquidity due to the curtailment of economic activities. The exceptions were the PRC and Singapore, which both saw increases in their respective government bond turnover ratios in Q2 2020. The PRC was one of the few markets that showed an economic recovery in 2020, which had a positive impact on investor sentiment. Also, notable is that nearly all markets posted steady declines in government turnover ratios from Q2 2020 to the fourth quarter (Q4) of 2020, except for Indonesia and Malaysia. In Indonesia, declining interest rates and renewed foreign investor interest helped boost liquidity. In Malaysia, the

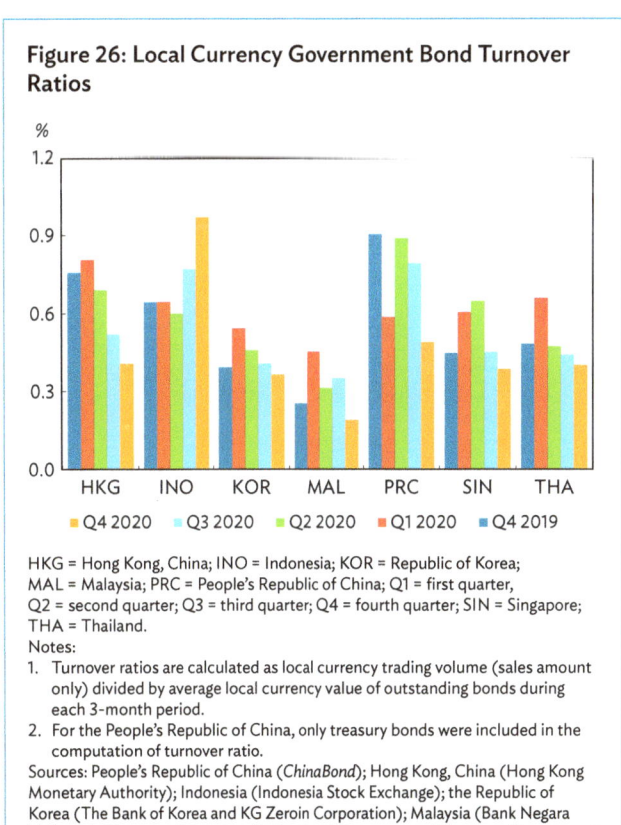

Figure 26: Local Currency Government Bond Turnover Ratios

HKG = Hong Kong, China; INO = Indonesia; KOR = Republic of Korea; MAL = Malaysia; PRC = People's Republic of China; Q1 = first quarter, Q2 = second quarter; Q3 = third quarter; Q4 = fourth quarter; SIN = Singapore; THA = Thailand.
Notes:
1. Turnover ratios are calculated as local currency trading volume (sales amount only) divided by average local currency value of outstanding bonds during each 3-month period.
2. For the People's Republic of China, only treasury bonds were included in the computation of turnover ratio.
Sources: People's Republic of China (ChinaBond); Hong Kong, China (Hong Kong Monetary Authority); Indonesia (Indonesia Stock Exchange); the Republic of Korea (The Bank of Korea and KG Zeroin Corporation); Malaysia (Bank Negara Malaysia); Singapore (Monetary Authority of Singapore and Singapore Government Securities); and Thailand (Bank of Thailand and Thai Bond Market Association).

government turnover ratio rose in the third quarter of 2020 as market sentiment improved with the easing of lockdown measures before plummeting in Q4 2020 as a resurgence of virus cases drove down investor confidence.

Survey respondents were also asked to provide their quotes for bid–ask spreads, which measure the difference between the buying and the selling price of a particular bond. A lower bid–ask spread indicates a more liquid market. The regional average bid–ask spread for on-the-run government bonds for the 2020 survey stood at 2.8 basis points (bps), which was unchanged from the 2019 survey (**Figure 27**).

The lowest government bond bid–ask spreads were found in the PRC and the Republic of Korea with bid–ask spreads of less than 1 bp each. The PRC has benefitted from continued development of its bond market as well as strong inflows from foreign investors. The Republic of Korea, on the other hand, is considered a safe haven among its emerging East Asian peers.

Bid–ask spreads narrowed in 2020 in four emerging East Asian markets: the PRC, Indonesia, Thailand, and Viet Nam. Bid–ask spreads in Viet Nam improved the most, falling to 4.5 bps in the 2020 survey from 5.5 bps in 2019, owing to strong domestic demand. The PRC's bid–ask spread also fell from 1.1 bps to 0.6 bps in the same period. The PRC and Viet Nam were the two markets in the region that successfully contained their COVID-19 outbreak early on, boosting investor sentiment in their respective markets. In contrast, Malaysia's bid–ask spreads worsened the most, rising to 4.0 bps in 2020 from 2.7 bps in 2019. The bid–ask spreads for all other emerging East Asian markets were marginally changed with either an increase or decrease of 0.3 bps or less.

Bid-ask spreads for off-the-run government bonds declined for the region as a whole, averaging 5.0 bps in the 2020 survey versus 5.5 bps in the 2019 survey (**Figure 28**).

Figure 29 presents the average transaction size for on-the-run government bonds in emerging East Asia. Changes in transaction sizes were mixed in the region. Large declines were noted in the PRC; Hong Kong, China; and Singapore; and to a lesser extent in the Philippines, while increases were seen in Malaysia and Indonesia. Based on the 2020 survey results, the Republic of Korea had the largest average transaction size at USD9.2 million per trade. The smaller markets of the Philippines and Indonesia had the smallest average transaction sizes at USD1.7 million each per trade.

Qualitative Indicators for Government Bond Markets

The second part of the liquidity survey delves into identified structural factors to assess the development

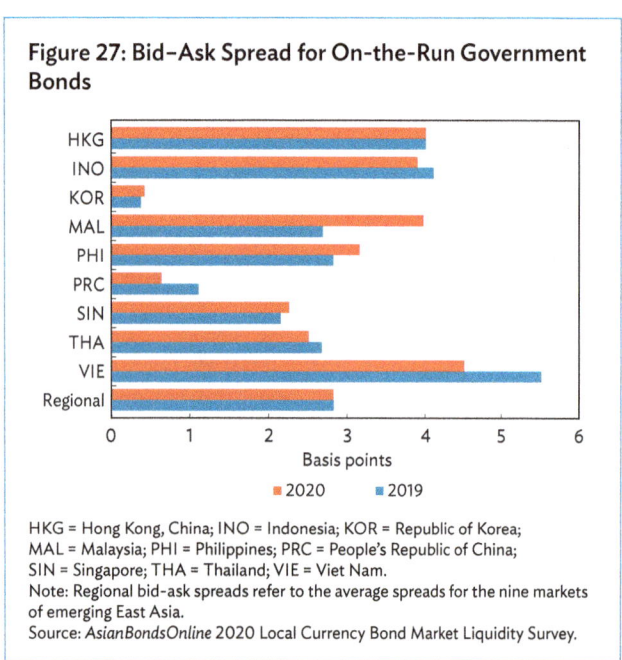

Figure 27: Bid–Ask Spread for On-the-Run Government Bonds

HKG = Hong Kong, China; INO = Indonesia; KOR = Republic of Korea; MAL = Malaysia; PHI = Philippines; PRC = People's Republic of China; SIN = Singapore; THA = Thailand; VIE = Viet Nam.
Note: Regional bid-ask spreads refer to the average spreads for the nine markets of emerging East Asia.
Source: *AsianBondsOnline* 2020 Local Currency Bond Market Liquidity Survey.

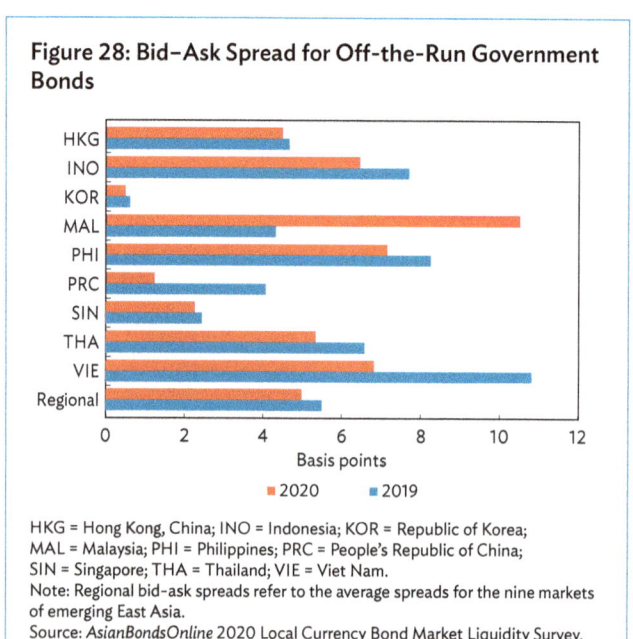

Figure 28: Bid–Ask Spread for Off-the-Run Government Bonds

HKG = Hong Kong, China; INO = Indonesia; KOR = Republic of Korea; MAL = Malaysia; PHI = Philippines; PRC = People's Republic of China; SIN = Singapore; THA = Thailand; VIE = Viet Nam.
Note: Regional bid-ask spreads refer to the average spreads for the nine markets of emerging East Asia.
Source: *AsianBondsOnline* 2020 Local Currency Bond Market Liquidity Survey.

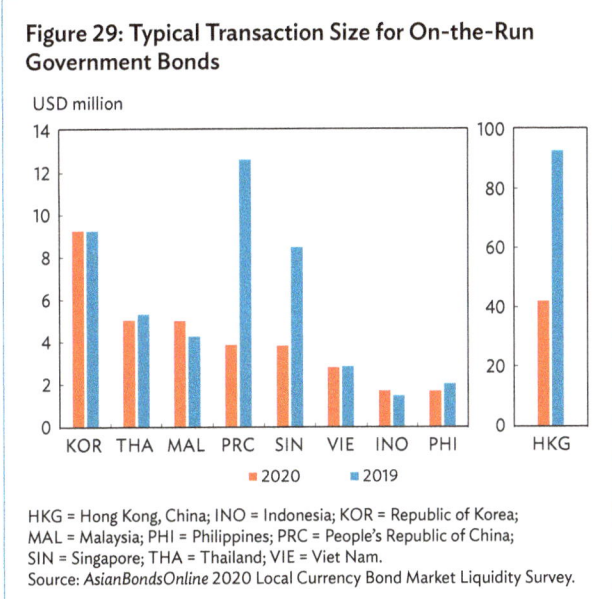

Figure 29: Typical Transaction Size for On-the-Run Government Bonds

HKG = Hong Kong, China; INO = Indonesia; KOR = Republic of Korea; MAL = Malaysia; PHI = Philippines; PRC = People's Republic of China; SIN = Singapore; THA = Thailand; VIE = Viet Nam.
Source: *AsianBondsOnline* 2020 Local Currency Bond Market Liquidity Survey.

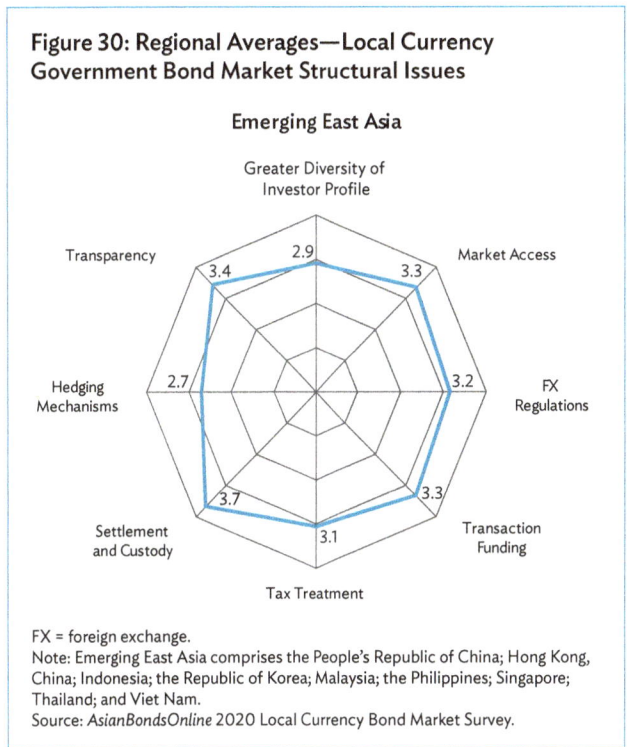

Figure 30: Regional Averages—Local Currency Government Bond Market Structural Issues

FX = foreign exchange.
Note: Emerging East Asia comprises the People's Republic of China; Hong Kong, China; Indonesia; the Republic of Korea; Malaysia; the Philippines; Singapore; Thailand; and Viet Nam.
Source: *AsianBondsOnline* 2020 Local Currency Bond Market Survey.

of each of the region's bond markets. Participants were asked to rate their respective markets based on a set of factors. A score of 3.0 or above for any structural factor is indicative of good development of the bond market in that particular area.

The qualitative survey results for 2020 were broadly similar with the 2019 results on average. Hedging instruments continued to score the lowest at 2.7, marginally higher than the previous period's score of 2.6 (**Figure 30**). Some participants cited limited ways of hedging government bond risk. For example, in Viet Nam, government bond futures were only launched in 2019, while in Indonesia, they were first offered in 2017. The Philippines currently lacks a bond futures market. Existing regulations also sometimes hamper the ability of financial institutions in the region to properly hedge.

Diversity of investors also scored a 2.9. In more developed emerging East Asian markets such as the Republic of Korea, a diverse array of investors is present, but in the Philippines and Viet Nam, active investors are mostly limited to a few financial institutions such as banks.

Market access, FX regulations, transaction funding, tax treatment, settlement and custody, and transparency all scored above 3.0, suggesting a high degree of development across the region. The highest score was for settlement and custody at 3.7, owing to modern developments in technology, thereby allowing for more efficient settlement processes in most emerging East Asian markets.

Transaction funding scored 3.3 for the regional average. The availability of funding sources for investors such as repo transactions are available in a number of emerging East Asian markets, but development is still lagging in markets such as the Philippines.

Tax treatment received a score of 3.1. In Hong Kong, China; Malaysia; and Singapore; tax exemptions or incentives are available for government bonds, resulting in higher scores for these markets for this structural factor. There are, however, some markets that still impose withholding taxes on government bond investments, including the Republic of Korea and the Philippines, translating into low tax treatment scores for each of them.

Quantitative Indicators for Corporate Bond Markets

Corporate bond markets in emerging East Asia tend to be less liquid compared to their government counterparts. In some economies, corporate bond markets are considered illiquid with very limited trading activities. In the 2020 survey, more participants noted an active secondary bond

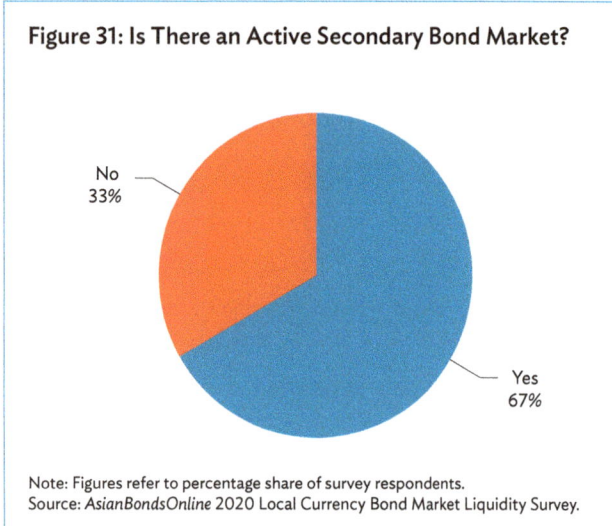

Figure 31: Is There an Active Secondary Bond Market?

No 33%
Yes 67%

Note: Figures refer to percentage share of survey respondents.
Source: *AsianBondsOnline* 2020 Local Currency Bond Market Liquidity Survey.

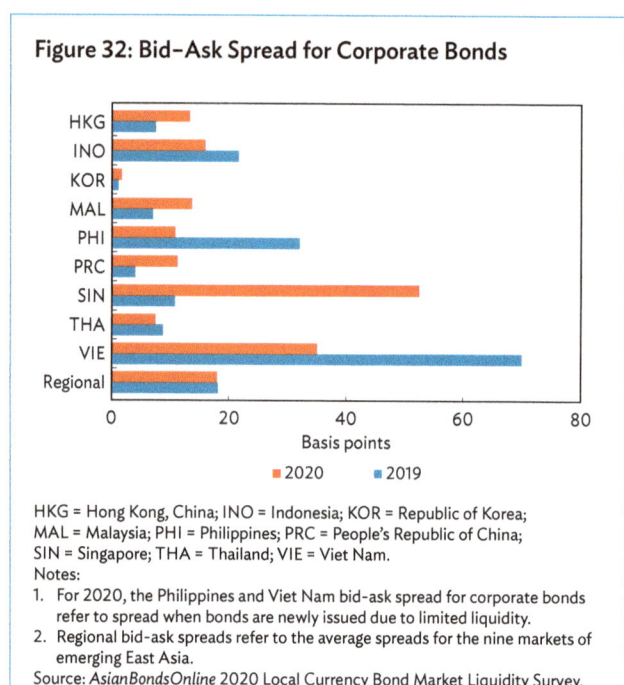

Figure 32: Bid–Ask Spread for Corporate Bonds

HKG = Hong Kong, China; INO = Indonesia; KOR = Republic of Korea; MAL = Malaysia; PHI = Philippines; PRC = People's Republic of China; SIN = Singapore; THA = Thailand; VIE = Viet Nam.
Notes:
1. For 2020, the Philippines and Viet Nam bid-ask spread for corporate bonds refer to spread when bonds are newly issued due to limited liquidity.
2. Regional bid-ask spreads refer to the average spreads for the nine markets of emerging East Asia.
Source: *AsianBondsOnline* 2020 Local Currency Bond Market Liquidity Survey.

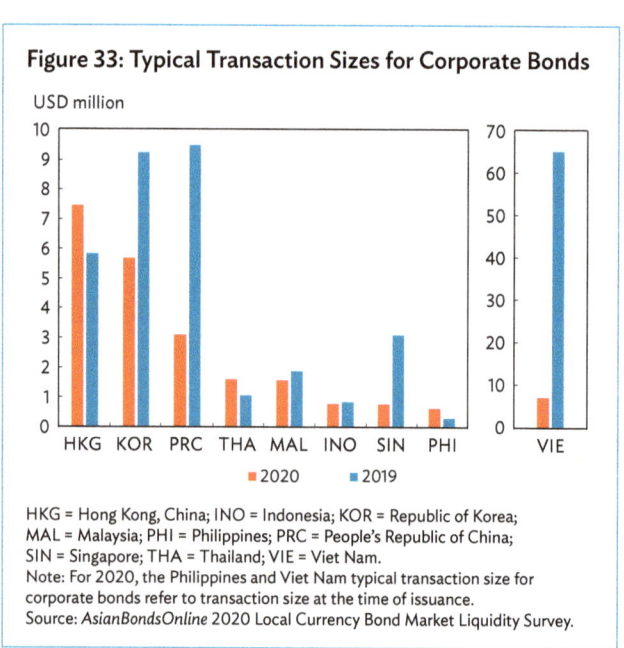

Figure 33: Typical Transaction Sizes for Corporate Bonds

HKG = Hong Kong, China; INO = Indonesia; KOR = Republic of Korea; MAL = Malaysia; PHI = Philippines; PRC = People's Republic of China; SIN = Singapore; THA = Thailand; VIE = Viet Nam.
Note: For 2020, the Philippines and Viet Nam typical transaction size for corporate bonds refer to transaction size at the time of issuance.
Source: *AsianBondsOnline* 2020 Local Currency Bond Market Liquidity Survey.

market in emerging East Asia compared to participants who said otherwise (**Figure 31**).

In terms of bid–ask spread for corporate bonds, the regional average was mostly unchanged at 18.0 bps in the 2020 survey from the 2019 average of 18.1 bps. Five out of nine emerging East Asian corporate bond markets saw a widening of bid-ask spreads as the pandemic outbreak highlighted bankruptcy concerns amid declines in economic output. Singapore had the largest widening of its corporate bid-ask spread, which rose to 52.5 bps from 10.8 bps (**Figure 32**). The PRC's bid-ask spread rose to 11.3 bps from 4.0 bps. Viet Nam registered the largest drop in its bid-ask spread, posting a spread of 35.0 bps in 2020 versus 70.0 bps in 2019, while the bid-ask spread in the Philippines fell to 10.8 bps in 2020 from 32.0 bps in 2019. For both Viet Nam and the Philippines, bid-ask spreads were based on the spread at the time of issuance as most market participants noted the absence of an active secondary market for corporate bonds. Compared with other markets in the region, Viet Nam and Singapore had the highest bid-ask spreads at 35.0 bps and 52.5 bps, respectively.

The typical transaction size for corporate bonds also significantly declined, with the regional average falling to USD3.2 million in the 2020 survey from USD10.7 million in the 2019 survey, due to a decline in corporate bond liquidity. Most markets had declines in their typical transaction sizes, but the largest declines were in Viet Nam (USD7.0 million in 2020 versus USD64.9 million in 2019), the PRC (USD3.1 million in 2020 versus USD9.4 million in 2019), and the Republic of Korea (USD5.6 million in 2020 versus USD9.2 million in 2019).

Indonesia, Singapore, and the Philippines had the smallest average transaction sizes, each with a typical transaction size of less than USD1.0 million (**Figure 33**). The largest average transaction sizes were in Hong Kong, China (USD7.4 million) and Viet Nam (USD7.0 million).

Corporate bond turnover ratios were mixed for the region. Only the Republic of Korea had fairly stable turnover ratios for each of the four quarters of 2020, ranging from 0.14 to 0.17 (**Figure 34**). In Thailand, corporate bond turnover ratios declined from Q1 2020 to Q2 2020, before posting a steady, albeit marginal, recovery in subsequent quarters.

In contrast, Malaysia's corporate bond turnover ratios were fairly consistent until the last quarter of 2020, where the turnover ratio fell to 0.03 from 0.06 in the third quarter of 2020. In the same period, Indonesia and Hong Kong, China saw improvements in their respective turnover ratios, reflecting increasing investor optimism in the last quarter of the year.

In the PRC, turnover ratios improved after Q1 2020, as an economic recovery was anticipated. Overall, corporate bond turnover ratios in the region were much lower compared to government bond turnover ratios.

Qualitative Indicators for Corporate Bond Markets

For emerging East Asia's corporate bond market, the region can be described as fairly well developed in terms of settlement and custody, FX regulations, transaction funding, and market access, with a regional average score above 3.0 in each of these categories (**Figure 35**). Settlement and custody is not a problem for most markets in the region, with a regional average of 3.4. Transaction funding also received an average score of 3.4. Market access had a score of 3.3, while FX regulations had a score of 3.2.

Figure 34: Local Currency Corporate Bond Turnover Ratios

HKG = Hong Kong, China; INO = Indonesia; KOR = Republic of Korea; MAL = Malaysia; PRC = People's Republic of China; Q1 = first quarter; Q2 = second quarter; Q3 = third quarter; Q4 = fourth quarter; THA = Thailand.
Notes:
1. Turnover ratios are calculated as local currency trading volume (sales amount only) divided by average local currency value of outstanding bonds during each 3-month period.
2. For the People's Republic of China, only treasury bonds were included in the computation of turnover ratio.
Sources: People's Republic of China (ChinaBond); Hong Kong, China (Hong Kong Monetary Authority); Indonesia (Indonesia Stock Exchange); the Republic of Korea (The Bank of Korea and KG Zeroin Corporation); Malaysia (Bank Negara Malaysia); Singapore (Monetary Authority of Singapore and Singapore Government Securities); and Thailand (Bank of Thailand and Thai Bond Market Association).

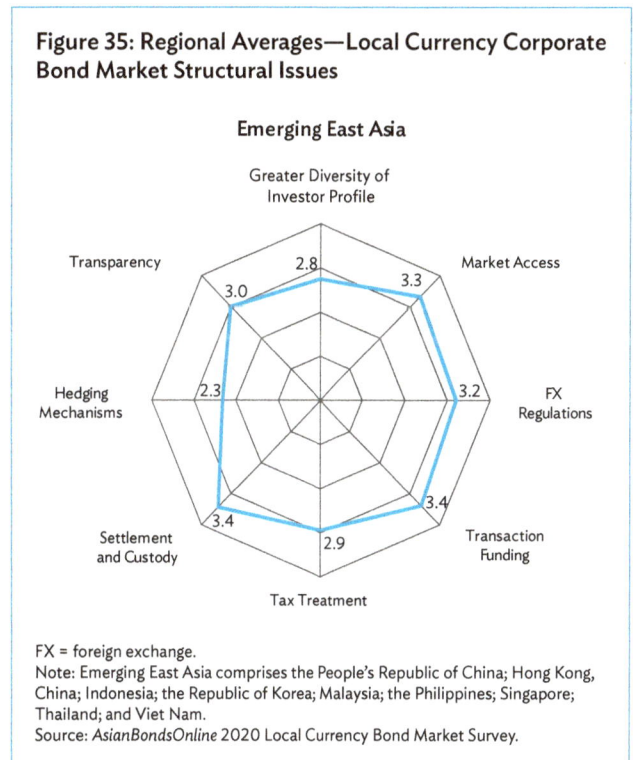

Figure 35: Regional Averages—Local Currency Corporate Bond Market Structural Issues

FX = foreign exchange.
Note: Emerging East Asia comprises the People's Republic of China; Hong Kong, China; Indonesia; the Republic of Korea; Malaysia; the Philippines; Singapore; Thailand; and Viet Nam.
Source: *AsianBondsOnline* 2020 Local Currency Bond Market Survey.

Market Summaries

People's Republic of China

The People's Republic of China's (PRC) local currency (LCY) bonds outstanding rose 3.3% quarter-on-quarter (q-o-q) in the fourth quarter (Q4) of 2020 after rising 5.4% q-o-q in the third quarter of 2020 to reach CNY101.4 trillion (USD15.5 trillion). Q-o-q growth in bonds outstanding slowed largely due to a decline in government bond issuance of 34.5% q-o-q, as local governments had largely completed their bond issuance in prior quarters. On a year-on-year basis, LCY bonds outstanding grew 20.5%.

Table 1: Size and Composition of the Local Currency Bond Market in the People's Republic of China

	Outstanding Amount (billion)						Growth Rates (%)			
	Q4 2019		Q3 2020		Q4 2020		Q4 2019		Q4 2020	
	CNY	USD	CNY	USD	CNY	USD	q-o-q	y-o-y	q-o-q	y-o-y
Total	84,185	12,090	98,178	14,457	101,413	15,537	2.8	14.1	3.3	20.5
Government	53,986	7,753	62,747	9,240	65,130	9,978	2.0	12.7	3.8	20.6
Treasury Bonds	16,698	2,398	19,327	2,846	20,933	3,207	4.6	11.9	8.3	25.4
Central Bank Bonds	22	3	15	2	15	2	57.1	–	0.0	(31.8)
Policy Bank Bonds	15,695	2,254	17,489	2,575	18,040	2,764	1.6	8.1	3.2	14.9
Local Government Bonds	21,571	3,098	25,915	3,816	26,142	4,005	0.4	17.0	0.9	21.2
Corporate	30,199	4,337	35,432	5,217	36,283	5,559	4.1	16.7	2.4	20.1
Policy Bank Bonds										
China Development Bank	8,704	1,250	9,415	1,386	9,771	1,497	0.5	6.8	3.8	12.3
Export–Import Bank of China	2,735	393	3,395	500	3,461	530	5.2	14.1	1.9	26.5
Agricultural Devt. Bank of China	4,256	611	4,679	689	4,809	737	1.8	7.1	2.8	13.0

( ) = negative, – = not applicable, CNY = Chinese yuan, LCY = local currency, q-o-q = quarter-on-quarter, Q3 = third quarter, Q4 = fourth quarter, USD = United States dollar, y-o-y = year-on-year.
Notes:
1. Calculated using data from national sources.
2. Treasury bonds include savings bonds and local government bonds.
3. Bloomberg LP end-of-period LCY–USD rate is used.
4. Growth rates are calculated from an LCY base and do not include currency effects.
Sources: CEIC and Bloomberg LP.

Total LCY corporate bond issuance in the PRC fell 4.4% q-o-q in Q4 2020 to CNY4.6 trillion. On a year-on-year basis, LCY corporate bond issuance grew 22.9%. A number of financial institutions issued perpetual bonds as part of their capital-raising efforts in Q4 2020.

Table 2: Notable Local Currency Corporate Bond Issuances in the Fourth Quarter of 2020

Corporate Issuers	Coupon Rate (%)	Issued Amount (CNY billion)	Corporate Issuers	Coupon Rate (%)	Issued Amount (CNY billion)
China Securities Finance[a]			Industrial Bank[a]		
1-year bond	3.85	20.0	Perpetual Bond	4.70	20.0
1-year bond	3.68	20.0	Perpetual Bond	4.55	30.0
1-year bond	3.60	20.0	Shanghai Pudong Development Bank[a]		
1-year bond	4.00	20.0	Perpetual Bond	4.00	2.5
1-year bond	3.90	20.0	Perpetual Bond	3.93	2.5
1-year bond	3.95	20.0	Perpetual Bond	4.07	2.4
1-year bond	4.10	2.0	Perpetual Bond	3.89	2.3
China State Railway Group[a]			Perpetual Bond	3.77	2.3
1-year bond	3.16	15.0	Perpetual Bond	4.04	2.2
5-year bond	3.47	15.0	Perpetual Bond	3.84	2.0
5-year bond	3.47	15.0	Perpetual Bond	4.35	2.0
5-year bond	3.45	15.0	Perpetual Bond	4.04	2.0
20-year bond	4.03	5.0	Perpetual Bond	3.77	2.0
20-year bond	4.04	5.0	Perpetual Bond	3.85	2.0
20-year bond	4.03	5.0	Perpetual Bond	4.15	1.9
Shanghai Pudong Development Bank			Perpetual Bond	4.25	1.8
Perpetual Bond	4.75	50.0	Perpetual Bond	3.85	1.5

CNY = Chinese yuan.
[a] Multiple issuance of the same tenor indicates issuance on different dates.
Source: Bloomberg LP.

By the end of December 2020, the total amount of LCY corporate bonds outstanding among the PRC's top 30 issuers reached CNY8.9 trillion, which comprised 24.6% of the total LCY corporate bond market. China Railway remained the dominant issuer with total bonds outstanding of CNY2.2 trillion, while the Agricultural Bank of China was a distant second with CNY0.6 trillion of bonds outstanding.

Table 3: Top 30 Issuers of Local Currency Corporate Bonds in the People's Republic of China

	Issuers	Outstanding Amount		State-Owned	Listed Company	Type of Industry
		LCY Bonds (CNY billion)	LCY Bonds (USD billion)			
1.	China Railway	2,173.5	333.0	Yes	No	Transportation
2.	Agricultural Bank of China	645.1	98.8	Yes	Yes	Banking
3.	Bank of China	530.6	81.3	Yes	Yes	Banking
4.	Industrial and Commercial Bank of China	517.3	79.3	Yes	Yes	Banking
5.	Central Huijin Investment	449.0	68.8	Yes	No	Asset Management
6.	Bank of Communications	391.6	60.0	No	Yes	Banking
7.	Shanghai Pudong Development Bank	340.7	52.2	No	Yes	Banking
8.	China Construction Bank	307.1	47.0	Yes	Yes	Banking
9.	China National Petroleum	274.9	42.1	Yes	No	Energy
10.	Industrial Bank	273.2	41.9	No	Yes	Banking
11.	China Minsheng Banking	264.0	40.4	No	Yes	Banking
12.	State Grid Corporation of China	261.5	40.1	Yes	No	Public Utilities
13.	China CITIC Bank	223.0	34.2	No	Yes	Banking
14.	State Power Investment	193.6	29.7	Yes	No	Energy
15.	Ping An Bank	178.7	27.4	No	Yes	Banking
16.	Tianjin Infrastructure Construction and Investment Group	159.0	24.4	Yes	No	Industrial
17.	Postal Savings Bank of China	155.0	23.7	Yes	Yes	Banking
18.	PetroChina	153.0	23.4	Yes	Yes	Energy
19.	China Southern Power Grid	153.0	23.4	Yes	No	Energy
20.	Huaxia Bank	143.0	21.9	Yes	No	Banking
21.	China Everbright Bank	141.8	21.7	Yes	Yes	Banking
22.	China Merchants Bank	139.2	21.3	Yes	Yes	Banking
23.	Shaanxi Coal and Chemical Industry Group	132.5	20.3	Yes	No	Energy
24.	Datong Coal Mine Group	123.4	18.9	Yes	No	Coal
25.	China Three Gorges Corporation	106.0	16.2	Yes	No	Power
26.	CITIC Securities	105.2	16.1	Yes	Yes	Brokerage
27.	China Datang	105.1	16.1	Yes	Yes	Energy
28.	Bank of Beijing	102.9	15.8	No	Yes	Banking
29.	Shougang Group	100.0	15.3	Yes	No	Steel
30.	Bank of Ningbo	99.1	15.2	No	Yes	Banking
Total Top 30 LCY Corporate Issuers		8,941.8	1,369.9			
Total LCY Corporate Bonds		36,282.7	5,558.7			
Top 30 as % of Total LCY Corporate Bonds		24.6%	24.6%			

CNY = Chinese yuan, LCY = local currency, USD = United States dollar.
Notes:
1. Data as of 31 December 2020.
2. State-owned firms are defined as those in which the government has more than a 50% ownership stake.
Source: *AsianBondsOnline* calculations based on Bloomberg LP data.

Hong Kong, China

The outstanding stock of local currency (LCY) bonds in Hong Kong, China reached HKD2,394.5 billion (USD308.8 billion) at the end of the fourth quarter (Q4) of 2020, rising 4.7% quarter-on-quarter (q-o-q) and 5.7% year-on-year. Growth rose more than fivefold in Q4 2020 from 0.9% q-o-q in the third quarter (Q3) of 2020, bolstered by faster growth in both government and corporate bonds.

Table 1: Size and Composition of the Local Currency Bond Market in Hong Kong, China

	Outstanding Amount (billion)						Growth Rate (%)			
	Q4 2019		Q3 2020		Q4 2020		Q4 2019		Q4 2020	
	HKD	USD	HKD	USD	HKD	USD	q-o-q	y-o-y	q-o-q	y-o-y
Total	2,266	291	2,287	295	2,395	309	0.1	1.8	4.7	5.7
Government	1,182	152	1,158	149	1,185	153	1.0	1.2	2.3	0.2
Exchange Fund Bills	1,055	135	1,042	134	1,043	135	0.7	2.4	0.1	(1.2)
Exchange Fund Notes	27	3	26	3	25	3	(6.3)	(17.4)	(3.1)	(6.0)
HKSAR Bonds	100	13	90	12	117	15	6.9	(5.4)	30.1	16.3
Corporate	1,084	139	1,129	146	1,210	156	(0.9)	2.6	7.1	11.6

( ) = negative, HKD = Hong Kong dollar, HKSAR = Hong Kong Special Administrative Region, LCY = local currency, q-o-q = quarter-on-quarter, Q3 = third quarter, Q4 = fourth quarter, USD = United States dollar, y-o-y = year-on-year.
Notes:
1. Calculated using data from national sources.
2. Bloomberg LP end-of-period LCY–USD rates are used.
3. Growth rates are calculated from an LCY base and do not include currency effects.
Source: Hong Kong Monetary Authority.

Issuance of LCY corporate bonds rose to HKD259.6 billion in Q4 2020 from HKD215.2 billion in Q3 2020. Growth rebounded to 20.6% q-o-q in Q4 2020 from a contraction of 8.2% q-o-q in Q3 2020. Among the top nonbank corporate issuers in Q4 2020, the largest issuer was state-owned Hong Kong Mortgage Corporation.

Table 2: Notable Local Currency Corporate Bond Issuances in the Fourth Quarter of 2020

Corporate Issuers	Coupon Rate (%)	Issued Amount (HKD million)
Hong Kong Mortgage Corporation[a]		
3-month bond	0.00	1.0
1-year bond	0.00	0.9
1-year bond	0.00	0.7
2-year bond	0.67	0.5
3-year bond	0.74	0.2
Airport Authority Hong Kong[a]		
7-year bond	1.36	1.0
7-year bond	1.55	0.6
10-year bond	1.90	0.7
10-year bond	1.95	0.7

Corporate Issuers	Coupon Rate (%)	Issued Amount (HKD million)
The Hong Kong and China Gas Company		
3-year bond	0.88	0.7
10-year bond	1.98	0.5
Hang Lung Properties[a]		
5-year bond	2.20	0.8
5-year bond	2.20	0.2
Sun Hung Kai & Co.[a]		
7-year bond	1.89	0.4
7-year bond	1.90	0.4

HKD = Hong Kong dollar.
[a] Multiple issuance of the same tenor indicates issuance on different dates.
Source: Bloomberg LP.

The outstanding bonds of the top 30 nonbank corporate issuers in Hong Kong, China amounted to HKD266.4 billion at the end of Q4 2020, accounting for 22.0% of the total LCY corporate bond market. Government-owned Hong Kong Mortgage Corporation remained the top issuer, with outstanding bonds amounting to HKD47.0 billion. Finance and real estate companies dominated the top 30 list in Q4 2020.

Table 3: Top 30 Nonbank Issuers of Local Currency Corporate Bonds in Hong Kong, China

	Issuers	Outstanding Amount		State-Owned	Listed Company	Type of Industry
		LCY Bonds (HKD billion)	LCY Bonds (USD billion)			
1.	Hong Kong Mortgage Corporation	47.0	6.1	Yes	No	Finance
2.	Sun Hung Kai & Co.	18.9	2.4	No	Yes	Finance
3.	The Hong Kong and China Gas Company	17.3	2.2	No	Yes	Utilities
4.	MTR	13.4	1.7	Yes	Yes	Transportation
5.	Link Holdings	12.9	1.7	No	Yes	Finance
6.	Hongkong Land	12.5	1.6	No	No	Real Estate
7.	New World Development	12.1	1.6	No	Yes	Diversified
8.	Henderson Land Development	11.2	1.4	No	Yes	Real Estate
9.	Hang Lung Properties	10.3	1.3	No	Yes	Real Estate
10.	Swire Pacific	10.3	1.3	No	Yes	Diversified
11.	Airport Authority Hong Kong	9.5	1.2	Yes	No	Transportation
12.	Hongkong Electric	8.5	1.1	No	No	Utilities
13.	CLP Power Hong Kong Financing	7.7	1.0	No	No	Finance
14.	Swire Properties	7.6	1.0	No	Yes	Diversified
15.	Guotai Junan International Holdings	7.2	0.9	No	Yes	Finance
16.	Wharf Real Estate Investment	6.9	0.9	No	Yes	Real Estate
17.	Smart Edge	6.8	0.9	No	No	Finance
18.	AIA Group	6.3	0.8	No	Yes	Insurance
19.	CK Asset Holdings	6.2	0.8	No	Yes	Real Estate
20.	Hysan Development Corporation	5.7	0.7	No	Yes	Real Estate
21.	The Wharf Holdings	5.1	0.7	No	Yes	Finance
22.	Future Days	4.2	0.5	No	No	Transportation
23.	Lerthai Group	3.0	0.4	No	Yes	Real Estate
24.	Cathay Pacific	2.5	0.3	No	Yes	Transportation
25.	China Dynamics Holdings	2.4	0.3	No	Yes	Automotive
26.	Champion REIT	2.3	0.3	No	Yes	Real Estate
27.	South Shore Holdings	2.2	0.3	No	Yes	Industrial
28.	Emperor Capital Group	2.2	0.3	No	Yes	Finance
29.	Emperor International Holdings	2.2	0.3	No	Yes	Finance
30.	IFC Development	2.0	0.3	No	No	Finance
	Total Top 30 Nonbank LCY Corporate Issuers	266.4	34.4			
	Total LCY Corporate Bonds	1,209.9	156.1			
	Top 30 as % of Total LCY Corporate Bonds	22.0%	22.0%			

HKD = Hong Kong dollar, LCY = local currency, REIT = real estate investment trust, USD = United States dollar.
Notes:
1. Data as of 31 December 2020.
2. State-owned firms are defined as those in which the government has more than a 50% ownership stake.
Source: *AsianBondsOnline* calculations based on Bloomberg LP data.

Indonesia

The local currency (LCY) bond market in Indonesia expanded to a size of IDR4,517.3 trillion (USD321.5 billion) at the end of December. Overall growth quickened to 10.0% quarter-on-quarter and 28.7% year-on-year in the fourth quarter (Q4) of 2020. The faster growth stemmed from the increased financing needs of the government to support stimulus measures and recovery efforts amid the coronavirus disease (COVID-19) outbreak.

Table 1: Size and Composition of the Local Currency Bond Market in Indonesia

	Outstanding Amount (billion)						Growth Rate (%)			
	Q4 2019		Q3 2020		Q4 2020		Q4 2019		Q4 2020	
	IDR	USD	IDR	USD	IDR	USD	q-o-q	y-o-y	q-o-q	y-o-y
Total	3,508,742	253	4,108,191	276	4,517,251	322	2.3	14.2	10.0	28.7
Government	3,063,641	221	3,667,452	246	4,091,542	291	2.4	15.2	11.6	33.6
Central Govt. Bonds	2,752,741	199	3,461,396	233	3,870,757	275	3.3	16.2	11.8	40.6
of which: sukuk	485,534	35	617,771	42	686,561	49	6.3	23.6	11.1	41.4
Central Bank Bonds	102,354	7	38,416	3	55,421	4	(12.2)	76.9	44.3	(45.9)
of which: sukuk	31,174	2	38,416	3	55,421	4	21.4	210.4	44.3	77.8
Nontradable Bonds	208,546	15	167,640	11	165,365	12	(0.6)	(10.6)	(1.4)	(20.7)
of which: sukuk	43,788	3	38,256	3	38,778	3	3.4	7.7	1.4	(11.4)
Corporate	445,101	32	440,739	30	425,709	30	1.7	8.1	(3.4)	(4.4)
of which: sukuk	30,123	2	30,915	2	30,341	2	(1.7)	41.4	(1.9)	0.7

( ) = negative, IDR = Indonesian rupiah, LCY = local currency, q-o-q = quarter-on-quarter, Q3 = third quarter, Q4 = fourth quarter, USD = United States dollar, y-o-y = year-on-year.
Notes:
1. Calculated using data from national sources.
2. Bloomberg LP end-of-period LCY–USD rates are used.
3. Growth rates are calculated from an LCY base and do not include currency effects.
Sources: Bank Indonesia; Directorate General of Budget Financing and Risk Management, Ministry of Finance; Indonesia Stock Exchange; and Bloomberg LP.

New issuance of LCY corporate bonds declined to IDR21.5 trillion in Q4 2020 from IDR37.4 trillion in the third quarter of 2020. Growth contracted 42.5% quarter-on-quarter and 37.1% year-on-year in Q4 2020. The decline in issuance coupled with an increase in maturities in Q4 2020 resulted in the LCY corporate bond stock to fall during the quarter.

Table 2: Notable Local Currency Corporate Bond Issuances in the Fourth Quarter of 2020

Corporate Issuers	Coupon Rate (%)	Issued Amount (IDR billion)	Corporate Issuers	Coupon Rate (%)	Issued Amount (IDR billion)
Indah Kiat Pulp & Paper			Permodalan Nasional Madani		
370-day bond	8.50	505	370-day bond	6.50	905
3-year bond	10.00	2,468	3-year bond	7.75	537
5-year bond	11.00	583	5-year bond	8.75	292
Sarana Multi Infrastruktur			Federal International Finance		
3-year bond	6.30	2,216	370-day bond	6.25	855
5-year bond	6.70	1,115	3-year bond	7.25	645
Wijaya Karya			Indonesia Infrastructure Finance		
3-year bond	8.60	331	370-day bond	5.00	570
3-year sukuk mudharabah	8.60	184	3-year bond	6.65	810
5-year bond	9.25	429	5-year bond	6.90	120
5-year sukuk mudharabah	9.25	159			
7-year bond	9.85	740			
7-year sukuk mudharabah	9.85	157			

IDR = Indonesian rupiah.
Note: Sukuk mudharabah are Islamic bonds backed by a profit-sharing scheme from a business venture or partnership.
Source: Indonesia Stock Exchange.

At the end of December 2020, the aggregate bond stock of Indonesia's 30 largest corporate bond issuers reached IDR309.7 trillion, accounting for a 72.7% share of total outstanding bonds. Leading the list were seven state-owned firms, with energy firm Perusahaan Listrik Negara in the top spot. More than half of the firms on the top 30 list were from the banking and finance industry.

Table 3: Top 30 Issuers of Local Currency Corporate Bonds in Indonesia

	Issuers	Outstanding Amount		State-Owned	Listed Company	Type of Industry
		LCY Bonds (IDR billion)	LCY Bonds (USD billion)			
1.	Perusahaan Listrik Negara	35,986	2.56	Yes	No	Energy
2.	Indonesia Eximbank	29,000	2.06	Yes	No	Banking
3.	Sarana Multi Infrastruktur	20,513	1.46	Yes	No	Finance
4.	Bank Rakyat Indonesia	20,144	1.43	Yes	Yes	Banking
5.	Sarana Multigriya Finansial	16,851	1.20	Yes	No	Finance
6.	Bank Tabungan Negara	15,975	1.14	Yes	Yes	Banking
7.	Bank Mandiri	14,000	1.00	Yes	Yes	Banking
8.	Bank Pan Indonesia	13,427	0.96	No	Yes	Banking
9.	Indosat	11,779	0.84	No	Yes	Telecommunications
10.	Waskita Karya	10,577	0.75	Yes	Yes	Building Construction
11.	Pegadaian	10,305	0.73	Yes	No	Finance
12.	Permodalan Nasional Madani	9,423	0.67	Yes	No	Finance
13.	Adira Dinamika Multi Finance	7,639	0.54	No	Yes	Finance
14.	Astra Sedaya Finance	7,313	0.52	No	No	Finance
15.	Semen Indonesia	7,078	0.50	Yes	Yes	Cement Manufacturing
16.	Telekomunikasi Indonesia	7,000	0.50	Yes	Yes	Telecommunications
17.	Bank CIMB Niaga	6,806	0.48	No	Yes	Banking
18.	Indah Kiat Pulp & Paper	6,747	0.48	No	Yes	Pulp and Paper
19.	Hutama Karya	6,500	0.46	Yes	No	Nonbuilding Construction
20.	Pupuk Indonesia	6,296	0.45	Yes	No	Chemical Manufacturing
21.	Federal International Finance	5,981	0.43	No	No	Finance
22.	Bank Pembangunan Daerah Jawa Barat Dan Banten	5,248	0.37	Yes	Yes	Banking
23.	Angkasa Pura II	5,000	0.36	Yes	No	Airport Management Serivces
24.	Mandiri Tunas Finance	4,878	0.35	No	No	Finance
25.	Bank Maybank Indonesia	4,849	0.35	No	yes	Banking
26.	Chandra Asri Petrochemical	4,589	0.33	No	Yes	Petrochemicals
27.	Adhi Karya	4,316	0.31	Yes	Yes	Building Construction
28.	Kereta Api Indonesia	4,000	0.28	Yes	No	Transportation
29.	Tower Bersama Infrastructure	3,788	0.27	No	Yes	Telecommunications Infrastructure Provider
30.	Medco-Energi Internasional	3,690	0.26	No	Yes	Petrochemicals
Total Top 30 LCY Corporate Issuers		309,695	22.04			
Total LCY Corporate Bonds		425,709	30.30			
Top 30 as % of Total LCY Corporate Bonds		72.7%	72.7%			

IDR = Indonesian rupiah, LCY = local currency, USD = United States dollar.
Notes:
1. Data as of 31 December 2020.
2. State-owned firms are defined as those in which the government has more than a 50% ownership stake.
Source: *AsianBondsOnline* calculations based on Indonesia Stock Exchange data.

Republic of Korea

The size of the Republic of Korea's local currency (LCY) bond market rose 1.2% quarter-on-quarter (q-o-q) to KRW2,633.2 trillion (USD2.4 trillion) at the end of December 2020, driven by growth in the corporate bond segment. Total outstanding LCY corporate bonds increased 1.4% q-o-q to KRW1,554.2 trillion in the fourth quarter (Q4) of 2020, as issuance of corporate bonds rebounded. Meanwhile, government bonds posted minimal growth of 0.9% q-o-q to reach KRW1,079.0 trillion as the rise in the stock of central government bonds was dampened by the decline in central bank bonds. On a year-on-year basis, the Republic of Korea's LCY bond market posted growth of 9.4%.

Table 1: Size and Composition of the Local Currency Bond Market in the Republic of Korea

	Outstanding Amount (billion)						Growth Rate (%)			
	Q4 2019		Q3 2020		Q4 2020		Q4 2019		Q4 2020	
	KRW	USD	KRW	USD	KRW	USD	q-o-q	y-o-y	q-o-q	y-o-y
Total	2,407,623	2,083	2,602,081	2,224	2,633,219	2,424	1.6	7.6	1.2	9.4
Government	951,912	824	1,069,062	914	1,078,982	993	(0.2)	4.2	0.9	13.3
Central Government Bonds	611,533	529	707,681	605	726,766	669	0.7	7.8	2.7	18.8
Central Bank Bonds	164,060	142	166,750	143	159,260	147	(4.0)	(4.4)	(4.5)	(2.9)
Others	176,319	153	194,631	166	192,956	178	0.3	0.6	(0.9)	9.4
Corporate	1,455,711	1,259	1,533,019	1,310	1,554,237	1,430	2.7	9.9	1.4	6.8

( ) = negative, KRW = Korean won, LCY = local currency, q-o-q = quarter-on-quarter, Q3 = third quarter, Q4 = fourth quarter, USD = United States dollar, y-o-y = year-on-year.
Notes:
1. Calculated using data from national sources.
2. Bloomberg LP end-of-period LCY–USD rates are used.
3. Growth rates are calculated from an LCY base and do not include currency effects.
4. "Others" comprise Korea Development Bank bonds, National Housing bonds, and Seoul Metro bonds.
5. Corporate bonds include equity-linked securities and derivatives-linked securities.
Sources: The Bank of Korea and KG Zeroin Corporation.

Issuance of corporate bonds in the Republic of Korea posted growth of 17.3% q-o-q to KRW143.4 trillion in Q4 2020 from KRW122.2 trillion in the previous quarter. The table below lists some of the notable LCY corporate bond issuances in the Republic of Korea in Q4 2020.

Table 2: Notable Local Currency Corporate Bond Issuances in the Fourth Quarter of 2020

Corporate Issuers	Coupon Rate (%)	Issued Amount (KRW billion)	Corporate Issuers	Coupon Rate (%)	Issued Amount (KRW billion)
Shinhan Bank[a]			Kookmin Bank[a]		
1-year bond	0.99	420	1-year bond	0.88	400
1-year bond	0.90	600	1-year bond	0.96	350
2-year bond	1.02	260	1-year bond	0.96	350
2-year bond	1.02	350	10-year bond	2.02	400
2-year bond	1.04	500	National Agricultural Cooperative Federation[a]		
2-year bond	1.05	500	2-year bond	1.00	170
2-year bond	1.03	550	3-year bond	1.09	250
Woori Bank[a]			5-year bond	1.47	140
1-year bond	0.89	400	5-year bond	1.49	400
1-year bond	0.90	400	Sinbo Securitization Specialty[a]		
1-year bond	0.90	400	3-year bond	1.26	402
2-year bond	0.99	500	3-year bond	1.31	512

KRW = Korean won.
[a] Multiple issuance of the same tenor indicates issuance on different dates.
Source: Based on data from Bloomberg LP.

The aggregate bonds outstanding of the top 30 LCY corporate issuers in the Republic of Korea reached KRW947 trillion, accounting for 60.9% of total corporate bonds outstanding at the end of Q4 2020.

Table 3: Top 30 Issuers of Local Currency Corporate Bonds in the Republic of Korea

	Issuers	Outstanding Amount		State-Owned	Listed on		Type of Industry
		LCY Bonds (KRW billion)	LCY Bonds (USD billion)		KOSPI	KOSDAQ	
1.	Korea Housing Finance Corporation	144,720	133.2	Yes	No	No	Housing Finance
2.	Industrial Bank of Korea	71,730	66.0	Yes	Yes	No	Banking
3.	Mirae Asset Daewoo Co.	66,854	61.5	No	Yes	No	Securities
4.	Korea Investment and Securities	60,689	55.9	No	No	No	Securities
5.	KB Securities	53,687	49.4	No	No	No	Securities
6.	Hana Financial Investment	51,880	47.7	No	No	No	Securities
7.	NH Investment & Securities	38,889	35.8	Yes	Yes	No	Securities
8.	Samsung Securities	31,556	29.0	No	Yes	No	Securities
9.	Shinhan Bank	29,042	26.7	No	No	No	Banking
10.	Korea Land & Housing Corporation	29,004	26.7	Yes	No	No	Real Estate
11.	Korea Electric Power Corporation	28,060	25.8	Yes	Yes	No	Electricity, Energy, and Power
12.	Shinhan Investment Corporation	27,022	24.9	No	No	No	Securities
13.	Korea Expressway	24,710	22.7	Yes	No	No	Transport Infrastructure
14.	The Export-Import Bank of Korea	23,485	21.6	Yes	No	No	Banking
15.	Kookmin Bank	21,944	20.2	No	No	No	Banking
16.	KEB Hana Bank	20,320	18.7	No	No	No	Banking
17.	Hanwha Investment and Securities	19,549	18.0	No	No	No	Securities
18.	Woori Bank	19,460	17.9	Yes	Yes	No	Banking
19.	Korea Rail Network Authority	19,130	17.6	Yes	No	No	Transport Infrastructure
20.	Shinyoung Securities	19,035	17.5	No	Yes	No	Securities
21.	NongHyup Bank	18,030	16.6	Yes	No	No	Banking
22.	Korea SMEs and Startups Agency	17,008	15.7	Yes	No	No	SME Development
23.	Meritz Securities Co.	16,682	15.4	No	Yes	No	Securities
24.	Shinhan Card	16,265	15.0	No	No	No	Credit Card
25.	Hyundai Capital Services	14,645	13.5	No	No	No	Consumer Finance
26.	KB Kookmin Bank Card	14,360	13.2	No	No	No	Consumer Finance
27.	Standard Chartered Bank Korea	13,360	12.3	No	No	No	Banking
28.	NongHyup	13,290	12.2	Yes	No	No	Banking
29.	Korea Gas Corporation	11,519	10.6	Yes	Yes	No	Gas Utility
30.	Samsung Card Co.	11,088	10.2	No	Yes	No	Credit Card
	Total Top 30 LCY Corporate Issuers	947,012	871.6				
	Total LCY Corporate Bonds	1,554,237	1,430.5				
	Top 30 as % of Total LCY Corporate Bonds	60.9%	60.9%				

KOSDAQ = Korean Securities Dealer Automated Quotations, KOSPI = Korea Composite Stock Price Index, KRW = Korean won, LCY = local currency, SMEs = small and medium-sized enterprises, USD = United States dollar.
Notes:
1. Data as of 31 December 2020.
2. State-owned firms are defined as those in which the government has more than a 50% ownership stake.
Sources: *AsianBondsOnline* calculations based on Bloomberg LP and KG Zeroin Corporation.

Malaysia

Malaysia's local currency (LCY) bond market expanded 1.3% quarter-on-quarter (q-o-q) and 8.0% year-on-year in the fourth quarter (Q4) of 2020, reaching MYR1,604.5 billion (USD399.1 billion) at the end of December 2020. LCY government bonds outstanding jumped to MYR852.6 billion on a 0.5% q-o-q increase that was led by central government bonds. LCY corporate bonds outstanding amounted to MYR751.9 billion at the end of December on growth of 2.2% q-o-q. A total of MYR1,016.3 billion worth of *sukuk* (Islamic bonds) was outstanding at the end of 2020.

Table 1: Size and Composition of the Local Currency Bond Market in Malaysia

| | Outstanding Amount (billion) | | | | | | Growth Rate (%) | | | |
| | Q4 2019 | | Q3 2020 | | Q4 2020 | | Q4 2019 | | Q4 2020 | |
	MYR	USD	MYR	USD	MYR	USD	q-o-q	y-o-y	q-o-q	y-o-y
Total	1,485	363	1,584	381	1,604	399	(0.5)	6.0	1.3	8.0
Government	773	189	848	204	853	212	(1.6)	4.7	0.5	10.3
Central Government Bonds	737	180	820	197	827	206	(1.5)	6.7	0.8	12.1
of which: sukuk	341	83	377	91	384	95	3.0	11.4	1.7	12.4
Central Bank Bills	9	2	4	1	2	0.5	(11.8)	(53.1)	(50.0)	(77.8)
of which: sukuk	1	0.2	0	0	0	0	(71.4)	(73.0)	–	(100.0)
Sukuk Perumahan Kerajaan	27	7	24	6	24	6	0.0	(5.6)	0.0	(10.1)
Corporate	712	174	735	177	752	187	0.7	7.6	2.2	5.6
of which: sukuk	569	139	592	142	609	151	1.8	12.7	2.8	7.0

( ) = negative, – = not applicable, LCY = local currency, MYR = Malaysian ringgit, q-o-q = quarter-on-quarter, Q3 = third quarter, Q4 = fourth quarter, USD = United States dollar, y-o-y = year-on-year.
Notes:
1. Calculated using data from national sources.
2. Bloomberg LP end-of-period LCY–USD rate is used.
3. Growth rates are calculated from an LCY base and do not include currency effects.
4. *Sukuk Perumahan Kerajaan* are Islamic bonds issued by the government to refinance funding for housing loans to government employees and to extend new housing loans.
Sources: Bank Negara Malaysia Fully Automated System for Issuing/Tendering and Bloomberg LP.

Total LCY bond issuance fell 0.3% q-o-q in Q4 2020 as issuance of LCY government bonds dropped 39.0% q-o-q to MYR31.5 billion. This was slightly offset by LCY corporate bond issuance soaring to MYR58.2 billion, an expansion of 51.8% q-o-q. Government-owned financing company Lembaga Pembiayaan Perumahan Sektor Awam and CIMB Bank were the two largest issuers of corporate bonds during the review period.

Table 2: Notable Local Currency Corporate Bond Issuances in the Fourth Quarter of 2020

Corporate Issuers	Coupon Rate (%)	Issued Amount (MYR billion)
Lembaga Pembiayaan Perumahan Sektor Awam		
3-year Islamic MTN	2.02	450.0
5-year Islamic MTN	2.35	500.0
7-year Islamic MTN	2.66	500.0
21-year Islamic MTN	3.82	1,500.0
22-year Islamic MTN	3.87	1,450.0
23-year Islamic MTN	3.91	1,350.0
CIMB Bank[a]		
10-year bond	3.15	50.0
10-year bond	3.15	2,450.0
Perpetual bond	3.60	550.0
Perpetual bond	4.00	200.0
CIMB Group Holdings[a]		
10-year bond	3.13	2,500.0
Perpetual bond	3.58	550.0
Perpetual bond	3.88	200.0
Malayan Banking		
10-year Islamic MTN	2.90	2,300.0
12-year Islamic MTN	3.10	700.0

MTN = medium-term note, MYR = Malaysian ringgit.
[a] Multiple issuance of the same tenor indicates issuance on different dates.
Source: Bank Negara Malaysia Bond Info Hub.

The outstanding LCY corporate bonds of the top 30 issuers amounted to MYR454.4 billion at the end of December 2020, or 60.4% of the total LCY corporate bond market. The government's Danainfra Nasional continued to top all issuers in terms of bonds outstanding in 2020, which also led to the finance sector topping all other sectors at the end of Q4 2020.

Table 3: Top 30 Issuers of Local Currency Corporate Bonds in Malaysia

	Issuers	Outstanding Amount		State-Owned	Listed Company	Type of Industry
		LCY Bonds (MYR billion)	LCY Bonds (USD billion)			
1.	Danainfra Nasional	72.3	18.0	Yes	No	Finance
2.	Prasarana	37.0	9.2	Yes	No	Transport, Storage, and Communications
3.	Cagamas	30.6	7.6	Yes	No	Finance
4.	Lembaga Pembiayaan Perumahan Sektor Awam	30.2	7.5	Yes	No	Property and Real Estate
5.	Project Lebuhraya Usahasama	29.4	7.3	No	No	Transport, Storage, and Communications
6.	Urusharta Jamaah	27.3	6.8	Yes	No	Finance
7.	Perbadanan Tabung Pendidikan Tinggi Nasional	24.1	6.0	Yes	No	Finance
8.	Pengurusan Air	18.2	4.5	Yes	No	Energy, Gas, and Water
9.	CIMB Bank	14.4	3.6	Yes	No	Finance
10.	Khazanah	14.2	3.5	Yes	No	Finance
11.	Sarawak Energy	13.0	3.2	Yes	No	Energy, Gas, and Water
12.	Maybank Islamic	13.0	3.2	No	Yes	Banking
13.	CIMB Group Holdings	12.6	3.1	Yes	No	Finance
14.	Malayan Banking	12.3	3.1	No	Yes	Banking
15.	Tenaga Nasional	10.0	2.5	No	Yes	Energy, Gas, and Water
16.	Jimah East Power	9.0	2.2	Yes	No	Energy, Gas, and Water
17.	Danga Capital	8.0	2.0	Yes	No	Finance
18.	Danum Capital	8.0	2.0	No	No	Finance
19.	Public Bank	7.9	2.0	No	No	Banking
20.	GOVCO Holdings	7.2	1.8	Yes	No	Finance
21.	Bank Pembangunan Malaysia	7.2	1.8	Yes	No	Banking
22.	GENM Capital	6.5	1.6	No	No	Finance
23.	YTL Power International	6.1	1.5	No	Yes	Energy, Gas, and Water
24.	Bakun Hydro Power Generation	5.9	1.5	No	No	Energy, Gas, and Water
25.	Telekom Malaysia	5.6	1.4	No	Yes	Telecommunications
26.	Turus Pesawat	5.3	1.3	Yes	No	Transport, Storage, and Communications
27.	EDRA Energy	5.1	1.3	No	Yes	Energy, Gas, and Water
28.	1Malaysia Development	5.0	1.2	Yes	No	Finance
29.	Jambatan Kedua	4.6	1.1	Yes	No	Transport, Storage, and Communications
30.	Kuala Lumpur Kepong	4.6	1.1	No	Yes	Energy, Gas, and Water
Total Top 30 LCY Corporate Issuers		454.4	113.0			
Total LCY Corporate Bonds		751.9	187.0			
Top 30 as % of Total LCY Corporate Bonds		60.4%	60.4%			

Notes:
1. Data as of 31 December 2020.
2. State-owned firms are defined as those in which the government has more than a 50% ownership stake.
Source: *AsianBondsOnline* calculations based on Bank Negara Malaysia Fully Automated System for Issuing/Tendering data.

Philippines

The Philippines' local currency (LCY) bond market grew 5.3% quarter-on-quarter (q-o-q) and 28.9% year-on-year to reach PHP8,567.7 billion (USD178.4 billion) at the end of December 2020. Government bonds outstanding totaled PHP6,955.5 billion at the end of the fourth quarter (Q4) of 2020, rising 7.0% q-o-q. In contrast, outstanding corporate bonds fell 1.3% q-o-q to PHP1,612.1 billion due to debt maturities and declining issuance in Q4 2020 compared with the previous quarter. Government and corporate bonds comprised 81.2% and 18.8%, respectively, of the LCY bond market at the end of December 2020.

Table 1: Size and Composition of the Local Currency Bond Market in the Philippines

	Outstanding Amount (billion)						Growth Rate (%)			
	Q4 2019		Q3 2020		Q4 2020		Q4 2019		Q4 2020	
	PHP	USD	PHP	USD	PHP	USD	q-o-q	y-o-y	q-o-q	y-o-y
Total	6,646	131	8,136	168	8,568	178	(0.8)	9.0	5.3	28.9
Government	5,141	101	6,503	134	6,956	145	(2.1)	7.5	7.0	35.3
Treasury Bills	486	10	876	18	949	20	(12.1)	(1.6)	8.3	95.3
Treasury Bonds	4,615	91	5,537	114	5,720	119	(1.3)	8.5	3.3	23.9
Central Bank Securities	–	–	50	1	220	5	–	–	340.0	–
Others	40	1	40	0.8	66	1	83.4	18.3	65.3	65.2
Corporate	1,505	30	1,633	34	1,612	34	4.0	14.5	(1.3)	7.1

( ) = negative, – = not applicable, LCY = local currency, PHP = Philippine peso, q-o-q = quarter-on-quarter, Q3 = third quarter, Q4 = fourth quarter, USD = United States dollar, y-o-y = year-on-year.
Notes:
1. Calculated using data from national sources.
2. Bloomberg end-of-period LCY–USD rates are used.
3. Growth rates are calculated from an LCY base and do not include currency effects.
4. "Others" comprise bonds issued by government agencies, entities, and corporations for which repayment is guaranteed by the Government of the Philippines. This includes bonds issued by Power Sector Assets and Liabilities Management (PSALM) and the National Food Authority, among others.
5. Peso Global Bonds (PHP-denominated bonds payable in US dollars) are not included.
Sources: Bloomberg LP and Bureau of the Treasury.

Corporate bond issuance totaled PHP59 billion in Q4 2020, down 53.3% q-o-q. Table 2 lists the notable bond sales during the quarter, led by China Bank with a PHP15.0 billion single bond issuance.

Table 2: Notable Local Currency Corporate Bond Issuances in the Fourth Quarter of 2020

Corporate Issuers	Coupon Rate (%)	Issued Amount (PHP billion)
China Bank		
2-year bond	2.75	15.00
SM Investments		
3.5-year bond	3.36	10.00
Union Bank of the Philippines		
3-year bond	2.75	8.12
Aboitiz Equity Ventures		
3-year bond	2.84	6.85
Filinvest Land		
3-year bond	3.34	6.34
Del Monte Philippines		
3-year bond	3.48	5.83

PHP = Philippine peso.
Source: Based on data from Bloomberg LP.

The outstanding LCY bonds of the top 30 corporate issuers at the end of December 2020 totaled PHP1,438.8 billion, which comprised 89.2% of the entire LCY corporate bond market. By sector, banks comprised the largest share at 43.7% on aggregate bonds outstanding of PHP628.6 billion. By issuer, property firm Ayala Land was the leader among the top 30 list with bonds outstanding amounting to PHP117.2 billion at the end of Q4 2020.

Table 3: Top 30 Issuers of Local Currency Corporate Bonds in the Philippines

	Issuers	Outstanding Amount		State-Owned	Listed Company	Type of Industry
		LCY Bonds (PHP billion)	LCY Bonds (USD billion)			
1.	Ayala Land	117.2	2.4	No	Yes	Property
2.	BDO Unibank	109.9	2.3	No	Yes	Banking
3.	Metropolitan Bank	104.0	2.2	No	Yes	Banking
4.	SM Prime Holdings	103.6	2.2	No	Yes	Holding Firms
5.	Bank of the Philippine Islands	86.1	1.8	No	Yes	Banking
6.	SMC Global Power	80.0	1.7	No	No	Electricity, Energy, and Power
7.	China Bank	71.2	1.5	No	Yes	Banking
8.	Security Bank	66.3	1.4	No	Yes	Banking
9.	San Miguel	60.0	1.2	No	Yes	Holding Firms
10.	SM Investments	58.3	1.2	No	Yes	Holding Firms
11.	Rizal Commercial Banking Corporation	55.3	1.2	No	Yes	Banking
12.	Philippine National Bank	52.2	1.1	No	Yes	Banking
13.	Maynilad	43.9	0.9	No	No	Water
14.	Vista Land	43.5	0.9	No	Yes	Property
15.	Petron	42.9	0.9	No	Yes	Electricity, Energy, and Power
16.	Ayala Corporation	40.0	0.8	No	Yes	Holding Firms
17.	Aboitiz Power	40.0	0.8	No	Yes	Electricity, Energy, and Power
18.	Filinvest Land	31.8	0.7	No	Yes	Property
19.	Aboitiz Equity Ventures	27.9	0.6	No	Yes	Holding Firms
20.	Philippine Savings Bank	25.4	0.5	No	Yes	Banking
21.	Robinsons Land	25.2	0.5	No	Yes	Property
22.	Union Bank of the Philippines	24.6	0.5	No	Yes	Banking
23.	San Miguel Brewery	22.0	0.5	No	No	Brewery
24.	East West Banking	17.7	0.4	No	Yes	Banking
25.	Robinsons Bank	16.0	0.3	No	No	Banking
26.	GT Capital	15.1	0.3	No	Yes	Holding Firms
27.	Doubledragon	15.0	0.3	No	Yes	Property
28.	San Miguel Food and Beverage	15.0	0.3	No	Yes	Food and Beverage
29.	PLDT	15.0	0.3	No	Yes	Telecommunications
30.	NLEX Corporation	13.9	0.3	No	No	Transport
Total Top 30 LCY Corporate Issuers		1,438.8	30.0			
Total LCY Corporate Bonds		1,612.1	33.6			
Top 30 as % of Total LCY Corporate Bonds		89.2%	89.2%			

LCY = local currency, PHP = Philippine peso, USD = United States dollar.
Notes:
1. Data as of 31 December 2020.
2. State-owned firms are defined as those in which the government has more than a 50% ownership stake.
Source: *AsianBondsOnline* calculations based on Bloomberg LP data.

Singapore

Singapore's local currency (LCY) bond market expanded 3.9% quarter-on-quarter (q-o-q) and 11.6% year-on-year in the fourth quarter (Q4) of 2020, reaching SGD502.9 billion (USD380.4 billion) at the end of December. LCY government bonds outstanding jumped to SGD329.5 billion on a 5.3% q-o-q increase as Singapore Government Securities bills and bonds, and Monetary Authority of Singapore bills rose during the review period. LCY corporate bonds outstanding amounted to SGD173.4 billion at the end of December on growth of 1.3% q-o-q.

Table 1: Size and Composition of the Local Currency Bond Market in Singapore

	Outstanding Amount (billion)						Growth Rate (%)			
	Q4 2019		Q3 2020		Q4 2020		Q4 2019		Q4 2020	
	SGD	USD	SGD	USD	SGD	USD	q-o-q	y-o-y	q-o-q	y-o-y
Total	451	335	484	355	503	380	2.6	13.1	3.9	11.6
Government	286	212	313	229	330	249	3.1	16.9	5.3	15.3
SGS Bills and Bonds	183	136	191	140	196	148	12.4	46.3	2.6	7.4
MAS Bills	103	77	122	89	133	101	(10.0)	(13.8)	9.4	29.3
Corporate	165	123	171	125	173	131	1.7	7.1	1.3	5.1

( ) = negative, LCY = local currency, MAS = Monetary Authority of Singapore, q-o-q = quarter-on-quarter, Q3 = third quarter, Q4 = fourth quarter, SGD = Singapore dollar, SGS = Singapore Government Securities, USD = United States dollar, y-o-y = year-on-year.
Notes:
1. Government bonds are calculated using data from national sources. Corporate bonds are based on *AsianBondsOnline* estimates.
2. SGS bills and bonds do not include the special issue of SGS held by the Singapore Central Provident Fund.
3. Bloomberg LP end-of-period LCY–USD rates are used.
4. Growth rates are calculated from an LCY base and do not include currency effects.
Sources: Bloomberg LP, Monetary Authority of Singapore, and Singapore Government Securities.

Total LCY bond issuance jumped 6.7% q-o-q in Q4 2020 to SGD216.6 billion as issuances of government bonds increased 7.2% q-o-q to SGD212.1 billion. This was slightly offset by LCY corporate bond issuances falling to SGD4.5 billion, a decline of 12.0% q-o-q. Singapore Airlines and the Housing & Development Board had the largest issuances during the review period.

Table 2: Notable Local Currency Corporate Bond Issuances in the Fourth Quarter of 2020

Corporate Issuers	Coupon Rate (%)	Issued Amount (SGD million)
Singapore Airlines		
5-year bond	1.63	850.0
10-year bond	3.50	500.0
Housing & Development Board		
15-year bond	1.30	600.0
CapitaLand Mall Trust		
12-year bond	2.15	250.0
Suntec Real Estate Investment Trust		
Perpetual	3.80	200.0
Starhill Global Real Estate Investment Trust		
Perpetual	3.85	100.0
Heeton Holdings		
3-year bond	6.80	70.3

SGD = Singapore dollar.
Source: Bloomberg LP.

The outstanding LCY corporate bonds of the top 30 issuers amounted to SGD88.4 billion at the end of December 2020, or 51.0% of the total LCY corporate bond market. The government's Housing & Development Board continued to top all issuers in 2020, which also led to the real estate sector topping all other sectors at the end of Q4 2020.

Table 3: Top 30 Issuers of Local Currency Corporate Bonds in Singapore

	Issuers	Outstanding Amount		State-Owned	Listed Company	Type of Industry
		LCY Bonds (SGD billion)	LCY Bonds (USD billion)			
1.	Housing & Development Board	25.4	19.2	Yes	No	Real Estate
2.	Land Transport Authority	9.5	7.1	Yes	No	Transportation
3.	Singapore Airlines	8.7	6.6	Yes	Yes	Transportation
4.	Frasers Property	4.0	3.0	No	Yes	Real Estate
5.	United Overseas Bank	3.3	2.5	No	Yes	Banking
6.	CapitaLand Treasury	3.1	2.3	No	No	Finance
7.	Mapletree Treasury Services	2.9	2.2	No	No	Finance
8.	Temasek Financial	2.6	2.0	Yes	No	Finance
9.	DBS Group Holdings	2.5	1.9	No	Yes	Banking
10.	Keppel Corporation	2.2	1.6	No	Yes	Diversified
11.	Sembcorp Financial Services	2.1	1.6	No	No	Engineering
12.	City Developments Limited	1.9	1.4	No	Yes	Real Estate
13.	Oversea-Chinese Banking Corporation	1.7	1.3	No	Yes	Banking
14.	Ascendas Real Estate Investment Trust	1.6	1.2	No	Yes	Finance
15.	CapitaLand Mall Trust	1.5	1.2	No	No	Finance
16.	NTUC Income	1.4	1.1	No	No	Finance
17.	Shangri-La Hotel	1.4	1.0	No	Yes	Real Estate
18.	Olam International	1.3	1.0	No	Yes	Consumer Goods
19.	GuocoLand Limited IHT	1.2	0.9	No	No	Real Estate
20.	CapitaLand	1.2	0.9	Yes	Yes	Real Estate
21.	Singapore Technologies Telemedia	1.2	0.9	Yes	No	Utilities
22.	Suntec Real Estate Investment Trust	1.0	0.8	No	Yes	Real Estate
23.	Public Utilities Board	1.0	0.8	Yes	No	Utilities
24.	Singapore Press Holdings	1.0	0.7	No	Yes	Communications
25.	Hyflux	0.9	0.7	No	Yes	Utilities
26.	Mapletree Commercial Trust	0.9	0.7	No	Yes	Real Estate
27.	DBS Bank	0.8	0.6	No	Yes	Banking
28.	Sembcorp Industries	0.8	0.6	No	Yes	Shipbuilding
29.	Wing Tai Holdings	0.8	0.6	No	Yes	Real Estate
30.	CapitaLand Commercial Trust	0.7	0.5	No	No	Real Estate
	Total Top 30 LCY Corporate Issuers	88.4	66.8			
	Total LCY Corporate Bonds	173.4	131.2			
	Top 30 as % of Total LCY Corporate Bonds	51.0%	51.0%			

LCY = local currency, SGD = Singapore dollar, USD = United States dollar.
Notes:
1. Data as of 31 December 2020.
2. State-owned firms are defined as those in which the government has more than a 50% ownership stake.
Source: *AsianBondsOnline* calculations based on Bloomberg LP data.

Thailand

Total local currency (LCY) bonds outstanding in Thailand fell 0.7% quarter-on-quarter (q-o-q) to reach THB13,923.5 billion (USD464.8 billion) at the end of the fourth quarter (Q4) of 2020. The contraction in LCY bonds outstanding was driven by negative q-o-q growth in both the government and corporate bond segments. The 0.3% q-o-q decline in government bonds outstanding in Q4 2020 reversed the 5.4% q-o-q growth posted in the third quarter (Q3) of 2020. Meanwhile, the 1.8% q-o-q drop in outstanding corporate bonds in Q4 2020 reversed the 1.1% q-o-q growth in the prior quarter.

Table 1: Size and Composition of the Local Currency Bond Market in Thailand

	Outstanding Amount (billion)						Growth Rate (%)			
	Q4 2019		Q3 2020		Q4 2020		Q4 2019		Q4 2020	
	THB	USD	THB	USD	THB	USD	q-o-q	y-o-y	q-o-q	y-o-y
Total	13,236	446	14,018	444	13,923	465	2.2	6.4	(0.7)	5.2
Government	9,451	318	10,260	325	10,232	342	2.5	5.2	(0.3)	8.3
Government Bonds and Treasury Bills	4,940	166	5,735	182	6,020	201	2.3	4.3	5.0	21.9
Central Bank Bonds	3,718	125	3,702	117	3,365	112	2.3	6.9	(9.1)	(9.5)
State-Owned Enterprise and Other Bonds	793	27	823	26	846	28	4.7	2.8	2.8	6.7
Corporate	3,786	127	3,758	119	3,692	123	1.6	9.4	(1.8)	(2.5)

( ) = negative, LCY = local currency, q-o-q = quarter-on-quarter, Q3 = third quarter, Q4 = fourth quarter, THB = Thai baht, USD = United States dollar, y-o-y = year-on-year.
Notes:
1. Calculated using data from national sources.
2. Bloomberg end-of-period LCY–USD rates are used.
3. Growth rates are calculated from an LCY base and do not include currency effects.
Source: Bank of Thailand.

New issuance of corporate bonds reached THB277.0 billion in Q4 2020, down from THB324.5 billion in Q3 2020. Growth contracted 14.6% q-o-q and 27.3% year-on-year amid weak investor confidence. Siam Cement led all issuers of new corporate bonds during the quarter, with total issuance amounting to THB25.0 billion.

Table 2: Notable Local Currency Corporate Bond Issuances in the Fourth Quarter of 2020

Corporate Issuers	Coupon Rate (%)	Issued Amount (THB billion)
Siam Cement		
4-year bond	2.80	25.0
ICBC Thai Leasing		
1-year bond	1.28	2.5
2.3-year bond	0.00	4.6
3-year bond	1.85	2.2
4-year bond	2.13	3.0
Bangkok Commercial Asset Management		
2.5-year bond	2.83	4.1
5-year bond	3.41	5.4
10-year bond	3.92	0.6
Indorama Venture		
5-year bond	2.78	4.0
7-year bond	3.15	2.0
10-year bond	3.42	3.0
BTS Group Holdings		
2-year bond	2.10	0.5
3-year bond	2.44	4.0
5-year bond	2.86	1.5
7-year bond	3.11	2.0
10-year bond	3.41	0.6

THB = Thai baht.
Source: Bloomberg LP.

The aggregate LCY bonds outstanding of the top 30 corporate issuers in Thailand amounted to THB2,155.4 billion at the end of December 2020, comprising 58.4% of the LCY corporate bond market. Siam Cement remained the largest issuer, with aggregate bonds outstanding amounting to THB175.0 billion. Food and beverage firms held the largest share of outstanding corporate bonds with an aggregate amount of THB389.4 billion.

Table 3: Top 30 Issuers of Local Currency Corporate Bonds in Thailand

	Issuers	Outstanding Amount		State-Owned	Listed Company	Type of Industry
		LCY Bonds (THB billion)	LCY Bonds (USD billion)			
1.	Siam Cement	175.0	5.8	Yes	Yes	Construction Materials
2.	CP ALL	173.1	5.8	No	Yes	Commerce
3.	Thai Beverage	170.3	5.7	No	No	Food and Beverage
4.	Bank of Ayudhya	123.8	4.1	No	Yes	Banking
5.	Berli Jucker	121.9	4.1	No	Yes	Commerce
6.	True Move H Universal Communication	115.8	3.9	No	No	Communication
7.	Charoen Pokphand Foods	109.7	3.7	No	Yes	Food and Beverage
8.	True Corp	104.3	3.5	No	No	Communication
9.	PTT	92.6	3.1	Yes	Yes	Energy and Utilities
10.	CPF Thailand	76.0	2.5	No	No	Food and Beverage
11.	Toyota Leasing Thailand	70.5	2.4	No	No	Finance and Securities
12.	Indorama Ventures	69.5	2.3	No	Yes	Petrochemicals and Chemicals
13.	Minor International	62.0	2.1	No	Yes	Hospitality and Leisure
14.	Bangkok Commercial Asset Management	54.2	1.8	No	Yes	Finance and Securities
15.	PTT Global Chemical	51.7	1.7	No	Yes	Petrochemicals and Chemicals
16.	TPI Polene	46.2	1.5	No	Yes	Property and Construction
17.	Global Power Synergy	45.0	1.5	No	Yes	Energy and Utilities
18.	Krung Thai Bank	44.0	1.5	Yes	Yes	Banking
19.	Banpu	43.6	1.5	No	Yes	Energy and Utilities
20.	Krungthai Card	43.6	1.5	Yes	Yes	Banking
21.	dtac TriNet	39.0	1.3	No	Yes	Communications
22.	Bangkok Expressway & Metro	38.7	1.3	No	Yes	Transportation and Logistics
23.	Muangthai Capital	38.6	1.3	No	Yes	Finance and Securities
24.	CH Karnchang	36.9	1.2	No	Yes	Property and Construction
25.	ICBC Thai Leasing	36.4	1.2	No	No	Finance and Securities
26.	Bangchak	36.0	1.2	No	Yes	Energy and Utilities
27.	TMB Bank	35.4	1.2	No	Yes	Banking
28.	Sansiri	34.7	1.2	No	Yes	Property and Construction
29.	Land & Houses	33.6	1.1	No	Yes	Property and Construction
30.	Mitr Phol Sugar Corp Ltd	33.4	1.1	No	No	Food and Beverage
Total Top 30 LCY Corporate Issuers		2,155.4	71.9			
Total LCY Corporate Bonds		3,691.9	123.2			
Top 30 as % of Total LCY Corporate Bonds		58.4%	58.4%			

LCY = local currency, THB = Thai baht, USD = United States dollar.
Notes:
1. Data as of 31 December 2020.
2. State-owned firms are defined as those in which the government has more than a 50% ownership stake.
Source: *AsianBondsOnline* calculations based on Bloomberg LP data.

Viet Nam

Viet Nam's local currency (LCY) bond market grew 8.1% quarter-on-quarter (q-o-q) and 31.7% year-on-year to reach VND1,640.8 trillion (USD71.0 billion) at the end of December 2020. Government bonds outstanding totaled VND1,358.3 trillion, rising 7.1% q-o-q in the fourth quarter (Q4) of 2020. Corporate bonds outstanding increased at a much faster rate of 13.6% q-o-q to VND282.5 trillion. Government and corporate bonds comprised 82.8% and 17.2% of the LCY bond market, respectively, at the end of December 2020.

Table 1: Size and Composition of the Local Currency Bond Market in Viet Nam

	Outstanding Amount (billion)						Growth Rate (%)			
	Q4 2019		Q3 2020		Q4 2020		Q4 2019		Q4 2020	
	VND	USD	VND	USD	VND	USD	q-o-q	y-o-y	q-o-q	y-o-y
Total	1,245,814	54	1,517,275	65	1,640,790	71	(3.8)	4.4	8.1	31.7
Government	1,141,009	49	1,268,599	55	1,358,315	59	(3.9)	5.4	7.1	19.0
Treasury Bonds	978,904	42	1,128,861	49	1,207,228	52	2.5	9.0	6.9	23.3
Central Bank Bonds	0	0	0	0	0	0	(100.0)	–	–	–
State-Owned Enterprise Bonds	162,105	7	139,738	6	151,087	7	1.5	(11.8)	8.1	(6.8)
Corporate	104,805	5	248,677	11	282,475	12	(2.8)	(5.5)	13.6	169.5

( ) = negative, – = not applicable, LCY = local currency, q-o-q = quarter-on-quarter, Q3 = third quarter, Q4 = fourth quarter, USD = United States dollar, VND = Vietnamese dong, y-o-y = year-on-year.
Notes:
1. Bloomberg LP end-of-period LCY–USD rates are used.
2. Growth rates are calculated from an LCY base and do not include currency effects.
Sources: Bloomberg LP and Vietnam Bond Market Association.

Corporate bond issuance in Viet Nam dropped 31.6% q-o-q in Q4 2020 to VND45.6 trillion due to the implementation of Decree No. 81/2020/ND-CP, which tightened regulations on corporate bond issuance effective 1 September 2020. Table 2 lists the notable bond sales during the quarter, led by Tuong Minh Investment and Real Estate Company Limited with a VND3.0 trillion single bond issuance.

Table 2: Local Currency Corporate Bond Issuances in the Fourth Quarter of 2020

Corporate Issuer	Coupon Rate (%)	Issued Amount (VND billion)
Tuong Minh Investment and Real Estate Company Limited		
5-year bond	Floating	2,950
Vietnam Technological and Commercial Joint Stock Bank[a]		
3-year bond		2,000
3-year bond		2,000
Becamex IDC Corporation		
5-year bond	5.80	2,000

VND = Vietnamese dong.
Note: Coupon rates for Vietnam Technological and Commercial Joint Stock Bank 3-year bonds are not available.
[a] Multiple issuance of the same tenor indicates issuance on different dates.
Source: Vietnam Bond Market Association.

Aggregate LCY bonds outstanding of the top 30 corporate issuers at the end of December 2020 amounted to VND188.1 trillion, which comprised 66.6% of the total LCY corporate bond market. More than half of the outstanding debt, amounting to VND102.4 trillion, came from the banking sector. The Bank for Investment and Development of Vietnam had the most bonds outstanding among the top 30 list with a total of VND20.7 trillion at the end of Q4 2020.

Table 3: Top 30 Issuers of Local Currency Corporate Bonds in Viet Nam

	Issuers	Outstanding Amount LCY Bonds (VND billion)	LCY Bonds (USD billion)	State-Owned	Listed Company	Type of Industry
1.	Bank for Investment and Development of Vietnam	20,670	0.89	Yes	Yes	Banking
2.	Masan Group	13,500	0.58	Yes	Yes	Finance
3.	Ho Chi Minh City Development Joint Stock Commercial Bank	10,748	0.47	Yes	Yes	Banking
4.	Tien Phong Commercial Joint Stock Bank	9,349	0.40	Yes	Yes	Banking
5.	Vietnam Prosperity Joint Stock Commercial Bank	9,150	0.40	Yes	Yes	Banking
6.	Lien Viet Post Joint Stock Commercial Bank	9,100	0.39	Yes	Yes	Banking
7.	Vietnam International Joint Stock Commercial Bank	9,050	0.39	Yes	Yes	Banking
8.	Vinhomes Joint Stock Company	8,890	0.38	Yes	Yes	Property
9.	Vietnam Joint Stock Commercial Bank for Industry and Trade	8,850	0.38	Yes	Yes	Banking
10.	Saigon Glory Company Limited	8,000	0.35	No	No	Property
11.	Sovico Group Joint Stock Company	7,550	0.33	Yes	Yes	Diversified Operations
12.	Orient Commercial Joint Stock Bank	7,535	0.33	No	No	Banking
13.	Asia Commercial Joint Stock Bank	5,300	0.23	Yes	Yes	Banking
14.	Vietnam Technological and Commercial Joint Stock Bank	5,000	0.22	No	No	Banking
15.	Bac A Commercial Joint Stock Bank	4,640	0.20	Yes	Yes	Banking
16.	Phu My Hung Corporation	4,497	0.19	No	No	Property
17.	Ho Chi Minh City Infrastructure Investment Joint Stock Company	4,390	0.19	Yes	Yes	Construction
18.	Nui Phao Mining and Processing Co., Ltd.	4,310	0.19	No	No	Mining
19.	Vinpearl	4,300	0.19	No	No	Hotel Operator
20.	NoVa Real Estate Investment Corporation JSC	4,207	0.18	Yes	Yes	Property
21.	Vingroup	4,000	0.17	Yes	Yes	Property
22.	Sun Ha Long Co., Ltd.	3,500	0.15	No	No	Property
23.	Vietnam Maritime Joint Stock Commercial Bank	2,999	0.13	Yes	Yes	Banking
24.	Tuong Minh Investment and Real Estate Company Limited	2,950	0.13	No	No	Property
25.	TNL Investment and Leasing Joint Stock Company	2,926	0.13	No	No	Property
26.	Phu Long Real Estate Joint Stock Company	2,800	0.12	No	No	Property
27.	Binh Hai Golf Investment and Development Joint Stock Company	2,745	0.12	No	No	Leisure
28.	Masan Resources	2,500	0.11	No	No	Manufacturing
29.	Hoan My Medical	2,330	0.10	No	No	Healthcare Services
30.	Refrigeration Electrical	2,318	0.10	Yes	Yes	Manufacturing
	Total Top 30 LCY Corporate Issuers	188,103	8.14			
	Total LCY Corporate Bonds	282,475	12.23			
	Top 31 as % of Total LCY Corporate Bonds	66.6%	66.6%			

LCY = local currency, USD = United States dollar, VND = Vietnamese dong.
Notes:
1. Data as of 31 December 2020.
2. State-owned firms are defined as those in which the government has more than a 50% ownership stake.
Source: *AsianBondsOnline* calculations based on Bloomberg LP data.

www.ingramcontent.com/pod-product-compliance
Lightning Source LLC
Chambersburg PA
CBHW040548220526

45473CB00017B/3053